ORGANIC
LIVING

IN **10** SIMPLE LESSONS

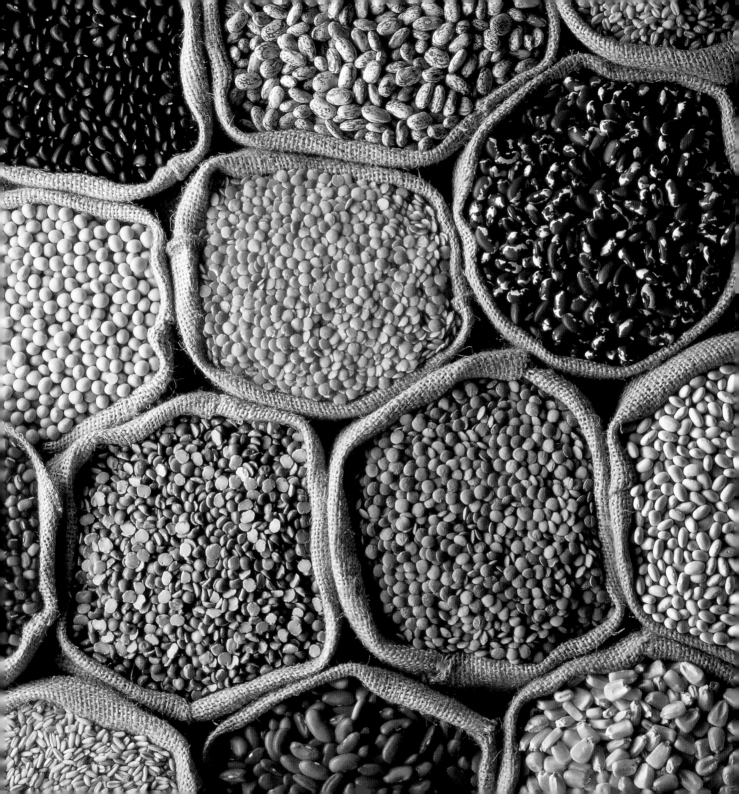

ORGANIC LIVING

IN 10 SIMPLE LESSONS

KAREN SULLIVAN

PIATKUS

For Cole and Luke

First published in the UK in 2001 by
Judy Piatkus (Publishers) Limited
5 Windmill Street
London W1T 2JA
e-mail: info@piatkus.co.uk

Conceived, designed and produced by
THE IVY PRESS LIMITED
CREATIVE DIRECTOR Peter Bridgewater
ART DIRECTOR Clare Barber
PUBLISHER Sophie Collins
EDITORIAL DIRECTOR Steve Luck
DESIGNERS Jane Lanaway, Keren Turner
PROJECT EDITOR Caroline Earle
COPY EDITOR Mandy Greenfield
PICTURE RESEARCH Liz Eddison
ILLUSTRATOR Madeleine Hardy

ISBN 0 7499 21951

PRINTED IN CHINA
by Hong Kong Graphics and Printing Ltd

CONTENTS

INTRODUCTION

Over the past decade there has been an unprecedented push towards an environmentally responsible and healthy approach to consumption. Far from being a hobby-horse for a few cranky individuals and organisations, this movement has gathered converts from all walks of life and from all areas of science and medicine. What is more, it has sparked the imagination of consumers worldwide. The result has been the biggest revolution in farming, manufacturing and consumption since the Second World War. That movement is called 'organic'.

Conventional farming methods are at the root of a large number of ecological, environmental and health issues, making the market ripe for the organic movement.

For most of us the word 'organic' means food. Organic food production has finally hit the mainstream, and with the twenty-first-century emphasis on health and well being, it could not have come at a better time. As long ago as the 1960s experts were expressing concern about what was going onto and into our food during its production. In 1962, for example, Rachel Carson's ground-breaking book *Silent Spring* warned that the use of pesticides would endanger human health and wildlife. In 1968 *Science* magazine published an article linking the decline of bird populations with reproductive failure due to pesticide accumulations. In 1975 the US Council on Environmental Quality stated that dairy and meat products accounted for over 95 per cent of the population's intake of the pesticide DDT. In 1989 the World Health Organisation estimated that one million pesticide poisonings occurred in the world each year, resulting in 20,000 deaths. And then we entered the 1990s, with BSE, salmonella, BST, 'gender-bender' chemicals, irradiation, genetic engineering – and more. As consumers responded with demands for change, the answer presented itself: going organic.

TAKING RESPONSIBILITY

The organic movement involves much more than simply avoiding the use of chemicals. Its aims are manifold, and they offer an answer to many of the woes of twenty-first-century life: pollution, farming crises, declining wildlife species, superbugs and pests, soil erosion, waste build-up, chronic health problems and even overfishing. The organic movement is responsible, which means that it is driven not by profit lines or quick-fix solutions, but by a genuine regard for the natural world. The original aim of organic farming was to create a system that depends upon the development of biological cycles, using crop rotation and making the most of natural fertilisers. Organic farmers rear animals naturally and with great concern for their welfare; they help to conserve the wildlife and habitats around their farms. Organic farming means using nature's own tools to do something natural: grow and harvest food that is safe for everyone and everything.

These aims are entirely consistent with the growing sense of responsibility that most consumers feel, and for that reason the organic movement has not only prospered, but has grown on an international level in a way that nobody could have predicted. Almost every country in the Western world now has an organic authority, with certification programmes cropping up almost as quickly as new organic products. Leading environmentalists around the world have set targets and prepared initiatives to encourage the growth of the movement. Organic is not a trend; it's a reality. However, it is important to look beyond questions of food to our lifestyle – and that is what this book is all about.

Growing crops naturally provides benefits for the environment, the consumer, wildlife and rural communities.

A PHILOSOPHY OF LIFE

Organic living means embracing the whole organic philosophy and making it part of our everyday life. From food, clothing, nutritional supplements and personal-hygiene products to dishwasher detergents, garden chemicals and furniture, there are organic options and safer alternatives. The chemical age is drawing to a close, and as we begin to realise just what effect our toxic heritage has had on our health and environment, we are choosing to dispense with the mindset encouraged by the major manufacturers and to go organic.

The benefits of going organic are now well-established, and as part of a healthy lifestyle, it can help to address a wide range of health problems.

Living organically does not involve giving up the pleasures of life, nor does it imply a wholescale lifestyle change. It simply means being a more responsible consumer. An awareness of the issues is the starting point, and that is where this book begins. No one can fail to be concerned about the issues raised by conventional farming methods, and it takes a very brave person to choose anything other than organic, once they know all the facts. When you have learnt how and why to choose an organic product, the rest is easy.

MAKING THE CHANGE

Most of us have busy, stress-filled lives, and the prospect of undertaking anything that involves some effort may seem rather daunting. However, making the change to organic living can be one of the most satisfying things you ever do. Your health will undoubtedly benefit, and many converts experience almost total relief from niggling symptoms such as digestive and skin problems, chronic colds, sleeping difficulties and nagging headaches. When you reduce your toxic load, your body functions more efficiently and you begin to both look and feel better.

Furthermore, choosing your food carefully and experimenting with different varieties, visiting farmers' markets or joining a box scheme, even just getting into the habit of reading food labels draws much-needed attention to the glories of our food and its importance in daily life. And because organic food tastes so much better, you will rediscover the joys of eating – and even cooking – well.

Organic gardening – whether you set up a single window box or devote the whole of your garden, creating a viable compost heap, using companion planting and mulches – is also enormously satisfying. You will enjoy the beauties of nature, and as wildlife begins to make your garden its home, you can experience the countryside in your own back yard. Your plants will flourish, and you will be able to relax and enjoy your creations (particularly if they are edible). What is more, your garden will be a safe, chemical-free place for your children to play in.

Think too about running a home where indoor pollution and toxic chemicals play no part in your daily life. By using organic products whenever you can, you will be creating a toxin-free sanctuary for your family. Your choices will have an impact on the environment and on the drive for animal-friendly, fair-trade products.

LOOKING TO THE FUTURE

Parents of young children are often the first to choose organic products over conventional, and there is a multitude of reasons why this makes sense. This book looks at why organic is important for children, over and above any other sector of the population. Apart from the obvious health reasons, going organic helps to preserve the world in which we live and make it a better place for our children to grow up in.

This book is all about change and responsibility. It is about taking on board the ideology of a movement that has now captured the world by storm. It is about caring enough about ourselves to make that change, which will affect not only ourselves and our families, but rural communities close to where we live and developing countries thousands of miles away. It is about enjoying a healthy, happy lifestyle that is in tune with the natural world, and about providing a sustainable future for everything that lies within it. When you choose to live organically you are taking part in a movement that holds the key to the future. Choose now, and be part of the solution.

Families with young children comprise one of the largest sectors of the organic market, and it's one way to help ensure a healthy future for the next generations.

1 WHAT IS ORGANIC?

'Organic' is a term that is defined by law, and anything that bears an organic label is governed by a very strict set of guidelines. Most countries in the Western world have set out stringent measures defining what can be labelled organic, and rigorous standards now cover everything from certification to food production, packaging and even distribution.

Organic agriculture is not a Western trend – countries all around the world are adopting its premises.

So what's the problem? First of all, the guidelines differ between countries, and not every country has a recognised regulatory system in place. This has led to concern that many imported organic foods may not meet our own standards. Second, organic has become big business, and there are cases of unscrupulous manufacturers trading on the word organic without fulfilling the criteria to do so. And with the growth of the organic industry, the number of regulatory agencies has increased. There are dozens of cases where products have failed to meet the standards of one certification body, only to be licensed by another.

Furthermore, the word organic has become synonymous with health, and not surprisingly consumers have been misled into believing that anything with an organic label is good for them. Controversy has recently erupted over the sale of 'unhealthy' organics, such as cigarettes and colas. Can something that is known to harm one's health actually be labelled organic? The answer is that indeed it can. The organic governing bodies are well aware of the effects of the consumer boom, and are becoming increasingly cautious about the products they are prepared to certify. Anyone given an organic certification is now required to keep detailed records ensuring full traceability from farm or production plant to the table.

WHAT DOES THE TERM
ORGANIC ACTUALLY MEAN?

In 1995 the National Organic Standards Board (NOSB) in the US defined organic as follows: 'Organic is an ecological production management system that promotes and enhances biodiversity, biological cycles, and soil biological activity. It is based on minimal use of off-farm inputs and on management practices that restore, maintain and enhance ecological harmony.'

When you buy organic, you are supporting a complete agriculture system that will affect the future of the world around us. Supporters of organic farming have emerged as a powerful voice against the introduction and use of farming methods that can damage health, wildlife, the environment and even the planet as a whole. Organic means more than just healthy eating and humane farming – it involves sustainable production and accountability. Sustainable farming involves ensuring that food needs are met, the environment is protected, the natural resources upon which the agricultural economy depends are maintained, non-renewable resources are used efficiently, the economic viability of farms is sustained, and the quality of life for farmers and society as a whole is enhanced. It's this all-encompassing approach that has drawn millions of advocates from around the world.

ORGANIC ADVANTAGES

Organic produce is grown with no synthetic chemical pesticides, no synthetic chemical fertilisers and with great attention paid to the health of the soils, animals and ecosystems that are involved in its creation. As a result, organic production offers the following benefits:

- It reduces the amount of toxic and persistent chemicals in our food supply. This will have a dramatic effect on overall health (see pages 34–35).
- It uses practices that eliminate polluting chemicals and reduce nitrogen leaching, thus protecting and conserving our water resources.
- It protects the health of future generations by creating long-term solutions to agricultural problems. The choices we make today will have a major impact on future generations.

- It encourages the protection of rural life.
- It creates a safer, healthier food supply.
- It improves the quality of the soil.
- It creates healthier habitats for both humans and wildlife. Organic agriculture places the balance of the ecosystem at the top of the priority list.
- It preserves a true economy. Organic food may seem to cost more, but conventional farming demands much more of society in terms of environmental and health costs.

AN ORGANIC HISTORY

The organic revolution is more of a renaissance than a revolution. Indeed, until the 1920s, all agriculture was, in general terms, organic. Farmers used natural means to feed the soil and to control pests, diseases and weeds. Food reached the table in much the same form as it left the farm.

In 1840 the German organic chemist Justus von Liebig published his famous work *Organic Chemistry in its Applications to Agriculture and Physiology*. He discovered that because plants consumed humus, it made sense to add humus to the soil in order to improve their growth. He analysed the chemical content of plants and argued that if such chemicals were added to the soil, then the plants' growth would be stimulated.

Under his influence practical agriculture changed dramatically. Companies began to manufacture 'superphosphate of lime' to add to compost piles to speed up decomposition and thereby greatly improved yields. In the 1870s these fertilisers were marketed as additions to compost piles, not as replacements for them. Together with mechanical help from reapers and tractors and the development of food-canning techniques, these additives encouraged a major surplus of food in the Western world for the first time in history.

It wasn't until the Second World War that farming methods changed dramatically. Many established farms still use the age-old practices that we now call 'organic'.

TOXIC SUBSTANCES

Manmade chemicals were not used in farming until the end of the nineteenth century, although the Victorians used some toxic chemicals, such as arsenic, mercuric chloride and nicotine, in order to control growth.

Wildlife has suffered the effects of broad-scale chemical use. One of the focuses of the organic movement is to ensure that natural populations are protected.

ORGANIC GARDENING

Other changes were also afoot. At the beginning of the twentieth century Sir Albert Howard, a colonial Brit living in India, reinvented the compost pile and methods to best use the natural resources of India. Over a period of 12 years he developed hundreds of strains of wheat and looked at proper soil drainage and irrigation that allowed wheat to be grown without the expense of fungicides. He discovered that crops grown in soils with a high organic content were more disease- and insect-resistant than the same crops grown with chemical fertilisers.

Above all, he shunned the fragmented approach of current agricultural research, which divided the soil, crops, livestock and humans into separate components. He believed that all of these comprised one complex system and that research into only one component – and into altering that component – would result in the rupture of the natural cycle of life and a dependency on artificial fertilisers and insecticides. For this reason Howard has been called the founder of organic gardening.

Many modern agriculturists discounted Howard's approach, and as the foundation of contemporary intensive farming took hold, so organic farming methods were discarded. But on a smaller scale the organic movement continued to grow. One of the best-known promoters was an American farmer called Jerome Rodale, who in 1940 began farming using Howard's theories. He founded the magazine *Organic Farming and Gardening* (now known as *Organic Gardening*) and, in 1950, *Prevention* magazine.

BIODYNAMICS

In Europe the first organic organisation was set up in 1929, based on the teachings of Rudolph Steiner, an Austrian scholar who was concerned that the fertility of Germany's land was being undermined by the use of chemicals.

The Bio-Dynamic Agricultural Association (BDAA, based in Europe, but now with offices in most countries, including the UK, Australia, New Zealand, South Africa and the US) uses Steiner's theory of biodynamics, which takes organic agriculture one step further, since biodynamic farmers – in addition to applying organic standards – use special preparations for field sprays, compost and manure treatments, and close attention is paid to practical rhythms in husbandry. Followers of biodynamics also pay special attention to companion planting, astrological timing, Steiner's special potions and the more spiritual interactions between people, plants and the universe. Biodynamic farmers and growers are now found in 38 countries around the world, and they use the symbol 'Demeter' (see page 16), an internationally recognised and respected accreditation.

The major change in farming methods can be traced very specifically to the Second World War, when research on chemicals designed as a nerve gas showed that they were also capable of killing insects. In 1939 the first of a new class of insecticides – chlorinated hydrocarbons – was developed as the answer to pest problems. They were toxic to most insect species, but were believed to cause little or no damage to plants and wildlife. Paul Müller, who was awarded the 1948 Nobel Prize for Medicine for his research, developed this insecticide, and in 1944 managed to prevent a winter typhus epidemic in Naples by killing the lice that carried the disease. He had, it was believed, found the perfect insecticide: DDT.

During the Second World War households on both sides of the Atlantic were encouraged to be self-sufficient and to grow as much

The long-term dangers of crop-spraying on local wildlife and on consumer health were first predicted by Rachel Carson in 1962.

food as possible. Britain's 'Dig for Victory' campaign, for example, urged people to grow their own fruit and vegetables, and many small-holdings sprung up in response. However, the use of chemicals was heavily promoted and a new way of farming was the result, leading to the outright dismissal of organic farming methods.

SILENT SPRING

In 1962 science writer Rachel Carson published *Silent Spring*, a book that created a public outcry. Carson criticised the indiscriminate use of chemical pesticides, fertilisers and weedkillers, citing case histories of damage already done. The book's title refers to the ultimate disappearance of songbirds, whose numbers had been diminishing, in Carson's view, because of the effects of the insecticide DDT. Her book helped to spawn environmental protection measures, and for the first time the public challenged the belief that the chemical industry knew what was best for us.

In the US the Vietnam War had changed public opinion about the 'official view', and the 'natural' approach now began to meet with some acclaim. The organic gardening movement became mainstream and farming was split into two distinct camps.

In Britain the organic movement had gathered pace in the 1940s, under the auspices of a Suffolk-based farmer, Lady Eve Balfour. Inspired by the work of Sir Albert Howard and Sir Robert McCarrison (a director of nutritional research in India, who had discovered a relationship between diet and health), she began to experiment at her own farm. She wrote the first book on organics, entitled *The Living Soil*. In 1946 she joined with several others to set up the Soil Association, and for the next 30 years Soil Association farmers and growers supplied organic food to specialised outlets.

Lawrence Hills, a well-known gardening journalist and one of the original founders of the Soil Association, created Britain's second organic organisation, known as the Henry Doubleday Research Association (HDRA), in 1958. He inspired hundreds of farmers to convert to organic methods, and today the HDRA, along with the Soil Association, sets the benchmark for organic standards worldwide.

GOING 'GREEN'

The 'be natural' approach of the 1960s and 1970s had an equal impact on both sides of the Atlantic. The focus on conservation and environmental issues, and the growth of the 'green' movement, encouraged farmers to adopt organic methods. While initially slow to take hold, the movement has grown apace since that time. Consumers have now begun to demand food and products that are organic, causing the greatest revolution in farming methods since the Second World War.

Today the demand for organic food is rising by 40 per cent, year on year, and the appeal for information about organic food and farming is increasing just as dramatically. With only 3 per cent of UK agricultural land turned over to organic farming (and only about one-fifth of 1 per cent in the US), there is considerable room for improvement. But the sector once dismissed as the pastime of crackpots and idealists has grown into a business worth some £4.6bn ($6.6bn) a year in the European Union and around £9.7bn ($14bn) worldwide. In any terms, that represents good business – and it's clearly on the increase.

Paradoxically, the need to be self-sufficient during the Second World War spawned a chemically dependent way of farming that has made us anything but.

NATIONAL SERVICE
WOMEN'S LAND ARMY

"GOD SPEED THE PLOUGH AND THE WOMAN WHO DRIVES IT"

APPLY FOR ENROLMENT FORMS AT YOUR NEAREST POST OFFICE OR EMPLOYMENT EXCHANGE

The Organic Food Federation, an independent group of producers at one remove from the food.

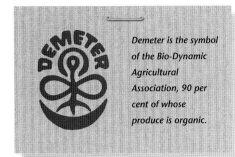

Demeter is the symbol of the Bio-Dynamic Agricultural Association, 90 per cent of whose produce is organic.

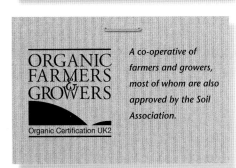

A co-operative of farmers and growers, most of whom are also approved by the Soil Association.

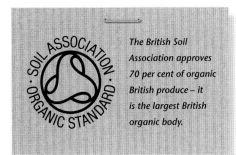

The British Soil Association approves 70 per cent of organic British produce – it is the largest British organic body.

ORGANIC STANDARDS

Organic standards are rigorous and cover every aspect of registration, certification, food production, permitted and non-permitted ingredients, the environment and conservation, processing, packaging and distribution. Standards are regularly updated and enforced by certification bodies around the world. Although they are not overseen on an international basis, the International Federation of Organic Agricultural Movements (IFOAM) lays down a series of standards that must be upheld within Europe and the UK. In the US, the USDA organic bill was passed in December 2000 and goes into force in February 2001, and will be fully implemented by August 2002. To date, only 31 states have certification programmes and the term 'organic' can only be used for goods produced under the authority of the Organic Foods Production Act (see page 118). The US organic industry is currently self-regulated, relying on third-party national certification organisations and state organic standards. To ensure quality products, consumers should look for the term 'certified organic'.

IMPORTED GOODS

Imported produce is subject to the same rigorous checks and guarantees, and it must come from countries recognised as applying equivalent standards and inspection procedures. If no national standards exist, specific producers will be inspected by recognised certification bodies to ensure that standards are being met.

WHAT'S THE DIFFERENCE?

Everything labelled organic has a set of rules defining its production (see in particular the first eight points on pages 24–25). Here's what makes these products different. All organic foods conform to the following specifications:

FRUIT AND VEGETABLES

◆ Artificial fertilisers and pesticides are banned from organic agriculture, and no genetic modification or irradiation is permitted (see pages 30–31).

◆ Tinned, bottled and frozen fruit and vegetables must conform to organic standards for production and packaging.

◆ Organic dried fruit does not contain sulphur dioxide, which is known to provoke extreme allergic reactions in some people.

DAIRY PRODUCE

◆ There are strict organic regulations covering all aspects of milk-producing and cheese-making, including the farming methods, animal welfare, livestock diet, transport, storage, manufacturing procedures and record taking.

◆ Chemical sprays are not used on the fields where the cows graze, which do contain genetically engineered crops. Cows are not routinely given antibiotics or other drugs. If animals do become ill, then homeopathic and herbal remedies are used in the first instance, and antibiotics only as a last resort. Milk is withdrawn from the market until antibiotic use has ceased.

◆ Organic milk can, by law, only come from dairy herds that are entirely organic.

◆ The diet of organic dairy cattle must be at least 60 per cent grass, and approved concentrates must be mainly (at least 85 per cent) of organic origin.

◆ Fewer animals are stocked on every acre of field, which means that there is no overgrazing.

◆ Organic cheese is made from organic milk and is free from artificial ingredients, such as colouring or flavouring.

◆ In organic cheese, the enzyme rennet (used to clot the protein in the milk) is not genetically engineered or animal-derived. It is made from naturally occurring fungi, which means that organic cheese can safely be eaten by vegetarians.

◆ Organic yoghurt, fromage frais, butter and cream are made from organic milk and are free from artificial ingredients.

◆ No organic dairy product contains BST (bovine somatotropin, see page 42).

MEAT

◆ Meat with an organic label is pure and safe.

◆ On organic livestock farms, chemicals that are routinely used in modern farming – such as artificial pesticides and fertilisers, GM (genetically modified) foodstuffs and growth-promoting agents – are not allowed.

◆ Organic animals are reared on organic land, and 70–90 per cent of their feed must be organic and free from fillers and animal matter. In other words, organic animals are not given offal to eat.

◆ Organic livestock must be raised non-intensively, with access to fresh air, exercise and daylight.

◆ Animal welfare standards are strict and give more protection to young animals, particularly in the area of live transport between farms. Winter housing must be provided in areas where weather conditions are severe.

◆ No cases of BSE (Bovine Spongiform Encephalopathy, see pages 32–33) have ever been recorded on an organic farm.

FISH

◆ The Marine Stewardship Council (MSC), an independent, non-profit-making international body, was set up to promote sustainable fishing practices worldwide. It will soon introduce a logo to identify fish derived from sustainable, well-managed sources.

◆ Organic accreditation bodies have set standards for pure, unadulterated fish, caught in ways that do not harm the ecosystem.

◆ An organic symbol for farmed fish has now been introduced by the Soil Association.

POULTRY

◆ Organic birds must conform to the strictest welfare standards.

◆ Flocks are smaller in size (the upper limit is 500 – commercial flocks are normally 3,000–15,000), which encourages good husbandry.

◆ Birds must have continuous, easy daytime access outdoors. Organic poultry must be free-range, which means they can wander outdoors instead of spending their lives in a cage. Debeaking is banned.

◆ The diet of organic birds must be at least 80 per cent organic. The other 20 per cent can be made up of pulses and elements such as soya. No animal protein (including fish) is permitted.

◆ All routine veterinary medicines are prohibited, except for the brief use (for chicks) of a medicine to control coccidiosis (a common infection in birds), which would otherwise affect their growth.

◆ Watch out: the word 'organic' is used indiscriminately in this area, so only buy birds from producers certified by a recognised board.

EGGS

◆ The debeaking of chickens is banned, and battery conditions and barn systems are not permitted.

◆ Hens must have a generous outdoor space and continuous, easy access outdoors.

◆ The maximum permitted flock size (to prevent stress) is 500.

◆ The pasture on which the hens feed must be rested for one out of every three years to prevent the build-up of parasites. At least 80 per cent of the birds' diet must be organically produced, while other feed must come from permitted natural sources.

◆ Preventative antibiotics, animal proteins, animals waste and yolk colourants are banned.

The plight of commercially reared farm animals has been one of the forces driving the organic movement, which focuses on animal welfare.

WINE

✦ Organic wine is produced without chemical fertilisers, herbicides (selective weedkillers) and synthetic pesticides, and no genetic modification takes place.

✦ Instead of chemically fertilising the soil, farmers look to restore the soil's balance by composting and adding a preservative.

✦ Vine varieties are chosen for their suitability to the environment and disease-resistance, not high yields.

✦ Older organic rules allowed the use of what is known locally as 'Bordeaux Soup' a copper-sulphate mix that works on contact with the leaves of the vine, but is not absorbed by the plant. However, recent regulations have led to the use of copper hydroxide, which has a much lower copper content, thereby minimising the amount of metals that are released into the environment. Many vine growers use herbs instead.

✦ Organic regulations also cover the amount of intervention allowed in the wine-making process, limiting the quantity of sulphites added and eliminating other additives.

SOFT DRINKS

✦ A minimum of 95 per cent of the ingredients of agricultural origin in organic soft drinks must come from certified organic sources (the remainder must come from a strictly controlled permitted list). This substantially reduces the number of additives that can be added to those soft drinks that are considered to be natural, organically produced and safe.

✦ Beware, however! Even organically produced sugar can rot teeth and cause weight gain, among other problems. Natural caffeine is no better for you than the real thing.

Organic vineyards are subject to strict standards, and prohibit the use of pesticides, fertilisers and fungicides. This benefits the environment too.

BREAD, PASTA AND OTHER GRAIN PRODUCTS

A minimum of 95 per cent (100 per cent in the US) of the ingredients (of agricultural origin) must be from certified organic sources. If a product says 'organic', it will be free of chemical pesticides, herbicides and other additives.

TERMINOLOGY AND LABELLING

The main organic certification organisations have established a series of terms in order to help consumers differentiate between the various products on the market.

These terms differ slightly between the European Union (EU), Australia and New Zealand and the US, but the main premises are the same in all: if you choose something that is certified organic, you can be sure that you are getting a natural, pure and unadulterated product. However, watch out for misleading 'soundalikes', such as 'organics', 'natural' and 'organically produced'. If a product does not have a certification symbol, along with the word 'organic' on the label, then it won't actually be organic.

THE LABELLING CONFUSION

Some of the terms used to describe eco-friendly products have some significance; others do not. It is important to remember, however, that these products are not organic. Here's what to look out for:

GREEN A 'green' product is less damaging to the environment, but it still is not organic unless it has a certification symbol.

FRIENDLY AND SAFE These terms create a wholesome image for a product, but if no further information is provided, it is impossible to tell whether or not the product really is less damaging to our environment.

RECYCLED If something is marked 'recycled' it means that it is made from, or contains, material that would otherwise have been waste; 'recyclable' simply means that it is technically possible to reuse material in the item. It does not guarantee that recycling will actually take place.

BIODEGRADABLE This means that a product breaks down easily and naturally. Look to see whether some or all of the ingredients are biodegradable, and how quickly this will occur.

NOT TESTED ON ANIMALS The "leaping bunny" logo guarantees to consumers that no animal tests were used in the development and production of a product. The logo is already in the marketplace in the United States and Europe, and was organised by the Coalition for Consumer Information on Cosmetics (CCIC).

ECOLABELS The European ecolabel and its identification number code indicate that a product has been independently assessed and has passed very stringent criteria.

Certification by a recognised organic body is a lengthy process, involving careful assessment to ensure that all of the strict criteria are satisfied.

consumption; there are therefore no restrictions on the use of the word 'organic' with respect to non-food products.

◆ For food labelled 'organic', at least 95 per cent of the ingredients of agricultural origin must come from certified organic sources.

◆ Manufacturers can claim that there are organic ingredients in a product, but only if between 70 and 95 per cent of the ingredients are organic. This does not allow them to call the product 'organic', but they can refer to the percentage of organic ingredients. This category requires certification, so look for a logo (see page 16).

ORGANIC LABELLING IN AUSTRALIA AND NEW ZEALAND

Neither Australia nor New Zealand has any domestic controls on the use of the words 'organic' or 'biodynamic', although Australia has had a National Standard for Organic & Biodynamic Food Production since 1992. This standard has enabled the Australian Quarantine Inspection Service (AQIS) to accredit organic and biodynamic certification organisations, on the basis of their ability to certify their growers as meeting the National Standard. Growers must demonstrate the application of a quality management system to the production of their organic or biodynamic foods. At present, New Zealand has no national standard, which has held up legislation to control the use of the word 'organic' on labelling.

In general, however, any AQIS-accredited certifier's kite-mark is confirmation that the product conforms to organic standards. These standards ensure that anything labelled organic contains at least 90 per cent organically produced ingredients.

ORGANIC LABELLING IN THE EU

◆ Farmers and growers must be certified and go through a two-year period of 'conversion' before they are legally able to market their goods as 'organic'. During their second year they can sell goods as 'approved organic conversion'.

◆ Animals and animal products do not have a conversion period during which they can be sold. They are either organic or not.

◆ The following require certification: food processors, manufacturers and packers – anyone who is processing, labelling or packing, marking their goods as organic or referring to organic ingredients on a label.

◆ Regulations do not apply to any goods that are not for human

WHAT IS ORGANIC?

10

QUESTIONS
& ANSWERS

Q Is Fair Trade the same thing as organic?

A No. Fair Trade standards are designed to ensure that disadvantaged producers – small farmers or plantation workers, for example – are given a fair deal in terms of trade, working conditions and prices. While the organic movement is heavily involved in social issues, it does not regulate this part of production as rigorously as it does growing and producing practices. Fair Trade products are not always organic, although those that carry an organic certification logo are. If Fair Trade issues are important to you, then you will need to see both logos in place.

Q Which products can actually be labelled organic?

A Not only fresh produce, but also packaged products, frozen foods, dairy products, meat, eggs and many other items grown and processed using organic standards can be labelled as certified organic. At the present time there is no official certification process for non-food goods, although in the UK the Soil Association is working to address this; in the US, however, the new USDA ruling does not extend to non-food goods.

Q Are organic products 'green'?

A By their very nature organic products are green – meaning friendly to the environment. Studies indicate that the industrialisation and globalisation of agriculture make a leading contribution to greenhouse gases. Organic farming methods reduce pollution of the environment by avoiding the use of artificial chemicals. They also reduce the use of non-renewable resources, such as petrol, which are employed to produce the fertilisers and other chemicals used in agriculture. Organic farming recycles natural resources, rather than stripping them.

Q Are organic products kinder to animals?

A Yes, without a doubt. In the UK the Soil Association insists upon stringent animal welfare standards, and all animals are reared in optimal conditions on organic farms. In the US the new USDA organic bill is set to include the same type of guidelines. Organic agriculture has a strong moral and ethical basis, which ensures that animals have access to fields, are allowed to express their natural behaviour, are given comfortable bedding and plenty of space. They are not fed drugs to artificially encourage growth or to make them 'perform' better.

Q How can I be sure that the eggs that are sold in my local store really are organic?

A *Eggs are one of the most commonly mislabelled food items, and some experts suggest that some 80 per cent of those labelled organic are, in fact, produced in battery conditions. The answer is only to buy eggs with an organic certification label that you trust. If your local shopkeeper can provide details of certification, the eggs should be fine. Remember, however, that free-range and barn-fresh eggs are not necessarily organic.*

Q Does a picture of a ladybird indicate that a product is 'green'?

A *Many products carry illustrations or symbols that promote a positive environmental image, often in green ink. Pictures of the planet, trees, flowers, endangered species or even organic-looking farming methods (a ladybird is a common ploy) do not mean that a product is kinder to the environment or has official approval. Look for positive information about how a product lives up to its 'green', 'eco-friendly' or 'kind to animals' image.*

Q Are organic products likely to contain more bacteria?

A *No. This has been a subject of some confusion because many people believe that composting is a breeding ground for bacteria. However, compost heat destroys the pathogens that are associated with bacterial food poisoning. Secondly, the majority of cases of bacterial infection involve animals that are intensively reared, or they are transmitted during handling. The organic market is strictly regulated to ensure that this type of transmission cannot take place, and organically reared animals do not live in conditions that cause bacterial infections.*

Q Why does some of the labelling say 'certified organic food' rather than just 'organic food'?

A *'Certified' means that the food has been grown according to the strict uniform standards that are verified by independent organisations. Certification includes inspection of farm fields and processing facilities, detailed record-keeping and period testing of soil and water to ensure that growers and handlers are meeting the set standards. Strictly speaking, anything with the label 'organic' should be certified (see page 16), so always make sure that there is a reputable organisation's logo on a product.*

Q Are organic products more perishable?

A *They ripen and go off more quickly, which can be a disadvantage if you shop only once a week or less often. However, you can be sure that you are eating food that is not artificially preserved, using chemicals and other methods, such as irradiation, which are at the root of many health scares. Furthermore, although conventional produce will last longer on the shelves, its nutritional value does diminish as time goes by. This means that your fresh produce may, in fact, be nothing of the sort. Organic produce goes off when it is genuinely past its best.*

Q How can I find out which additives are harmful?

A *Different countries allow different additives to be used in food production, and these change as more research becomes available. For technical advice, I recommend a website run jointly by the FAO (Food and Agriculture Organisation of the United Nations) and the WHO (World Health Organisation) Expert Committee on Food Additives (JECFA) at jecfa.ilsi.org. There is also an excellent section on food additives on the Center for Science in the Public Interest (CSPI) website: www.cspinet.org. Otherwise, look for a good book on the subject, such as E is for Additives.*

2 WHY GO ORGANIC?

Choosing to go organic means following a trend that can make a real difference to the health of the planet and everything within it. While there is still some controversy over claims that organic food is more nutritious (see page 26), there are undoubtedly other benefits, and these can have a wide-ranging impact on both your own health and that of your children. Many experts believe that organic farming is the only sustainable farming method for the future.

The full effects of agro-chemicals on our long-term health, immunity and fertility are still not completely understood, which makes it all the more important to preserve our children's health by choosing the organic alternatives.

WHAT ARE THE MAIN REASONS FOR GOING ORGANIC?

◆ Organic food is grown and produced under natural conditions, without the use of chemicals.

◆ Organic vegetables are grown without artificial fertilisers or pesticides, in ground that has been tested and declared free of contamination. This prevents the practice of intensive farming.

◆ Nothing labelled organic is irradiated, or contains any GM organisms (see pages 30–31).

◆ You avoid all the hundreds of additives (or E numbers as they are called in the EU) regularly found in conventional foods. Many additives are known to cause cancer, hyperactivity, insomnia, birth defects, anxiety, asthma and allergies.

◆ Organically raised animals are given comfortable surroundings, with sufficient space, and are fed food that has been organically produced. Land that is used for grazing must not have pesticides or any other chemicals sprayed on it.

◆ No antibiotics or other drugs are given to organically raised animals, unless they are genuinely ill (see page 17). They are not fed anything containing animal products, if they are natural herbivores, and most of their food is found in their natural environment – the fields of the farm.

✤ Organically raised animals are 'free-range', which means that they can wander outdoors instead of spending their lives in a stable or cage.

✤ No organic foods have ever been linked with BSE.

✤ Organic food is more than just a new trend in eating – it is the food of the future, and one of the few ways to eat safely and be certain that what you are eating is healthy.

✤ Intensive farming depletes the soil, creating a need for increasing amounts of fertiliser, which eventually makes its way into our food through the plants we eat and the animals that also eat these plants. Fertilisers are dangerous for a number of reasons (see pages 44–45).

✤ The antibiotics required to treat farm animals, and to boost their growth rates, can also enter our food chain and, through that, our bodies. More and more bacteria are becoming resistant to the antibiotics used, which creates a race to find even more drugs to treat the new strains of disease. The problem is that bacteria that are resistant to antibiotics can become impossible to treat.

✤ Certified organic food is grown and only minimally processed to strict national and international standards, which are routinely checked. The food is easily traceable and you can therefore trust the claims that are being made about it.

✤ Going organic increases the demand for organic products, which in turn sends a message to food manufacturers, farmers, retailers and governments that you don't want to buy intensively farmed food. This will make organic food more readily available and therefore less expensive.

The problem with many agricultural chemicals is that they do not fully discriminate. The chemicals designed to kill insects will do the same to wildlife and, in larger doses, humans.

✤ Sustainable farming is the only way that we can preserve our natural resources. Organic production builds up the health and fertility of the soil with composts, green manures and cover crops, and with crop rotation.

✤ Pollution caused by intensive farming is reduced. Such pollution contaminates ground-water, rivers, streams and lakes with nitrates, pesticides and drugs. By its nature, organic farming preserves rather than uses the earth's natural resources, leading to a reduced dependence on non-renewable resources, such as fossil fuels.

✤ Organic production both protects and encourages wildlife (see page 67) and their habitats, which have been gradually destroyed by intensive farming; as a result, dozens of species are now extinct.

✤ Because you have a choice! Never before have we been given the opportunity to control what we eat and use on our bodies – take it before it's too late.

ORGANIC FOR HEALTH

One of the main reasons why increasing numbers of consumers are choosing organic products is for the sake of their health. In fact, a 1999 survey found that 60 per cent of those who opted for organic alternatives gave this as their main reason for doing so, while half also said that they were attracted by the lack of pesticides in organic products. Studies show that organic produce is healthier for a variety of different reasons, and the growing trend towards taking personal responsibility for our health has led to an unprecedented demand for organic products.

NUTRITION

Organic food is higher in vitamins, minerals and other nutrients required for optimum health. This has been an area of dispute over the past year, with some experts claiming that organic food is no better for us nutritionally, but just consider the following: if foods are grown naturally, ripened naturally by the sun (which increases their nutritional content), not sprayed with preservatives that allow them to sit for months in the backs of lorries or on supermarket shelves, and grown in soil that is naturally replenished, then we have a much better chance of getting the nutrition that we need from our food. And there is sound evidence to back that up (see The Facts on pages 28–29).

Studies show that organic produce contains between 50 and 100 per cent more minerals, and 25 per cent more fibre. In real terms, you get a lot more nutrition from organic food.

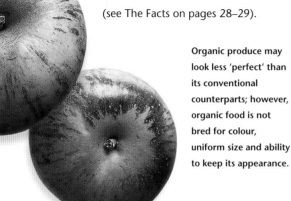

Organic produce may look less 'perfect' than its conventional counterparts; however, organic food is not bred for colour, uniform size and ability to keep its appearance.

Furthermore, much of the food that reaches our table has been irradiated. While irradiated food looks like fresh, raw food, its nutrient content is that of cooked food – in other words, substantially lower. Irradiation is legal for herbs and spices in the UK, but this may change in the near future. It is common in the US and used in some countries in the EU and in Australia. In the UK, it must be labelled 'irradiated' or 'treated with ionising radiation', but this labelling requirement does not apply to ingredients that make up less than 25 per cent of a labelled product. Organic food is not irradiated.

Patrick Holford, founder of the UK's Institute of Optimum Nutrition, has made another valid point, which is often ignored by the anti-organic lobbyists. He claims that foods containing high levels of toxic chemicals actually act as anti-nutrients, gradually robbing the body of nutrients that are vital for our general health and well being. In other words, the extra demands that are placed on the body by non-organic foods reduce nutrient levels, making us much more susceptible to illness.

FOOD SCARES

Food scares are undoubtedly at the root of many consumers' decision to go organic. BSE and GM foods (discussed later in the chapter), food-borne illnesses and other nasties dominate newspaper headlines on an almost daily basis, and not surprisingly we have become disillusioned by government assurances that all is well.

The fact is that many of the food scares that threaten public health are the product of intensive farming methods. The conditions in which animals and fowl are farmed create a breeding ground for disease. The overuse of antibiotics and other chemicals reduces the immunity of the animals, which means that they are more susceptible to diseases, including fungal infections, viruses and bacteria, which are passed straight on to the consumer. And because these animals are kept under such stress, many other drugs are required to keep them alive and growing.

In the UK, food-poisoning incidents have increased by 400 per cent in just ten years. At least two million people suffer from food poisoning each year, although an unpublished government report puts that figure nearer to nine million (because many cases are not reported). In the US, that figure is nearly 76 million. About 1.5 million Australians are affected by food poisoning each year. There are no documented cases of organic meat or poultry creating food-poisoning epidemics. According to government statistics, most non-organic beef cattle are contaminated with *E. coli* 0157:H7; over 90 per cent of chickens are tainted with campylobacter, and 30 per cent of poultry are infected with salmonella. An estimated 75 per cent of chickens sold in the EU are infected with salmonella.

A recent UN Food and Agriculture Organisation (FAO) report concluded that organic practices can actually reduce the *E. coli* infection that causes food poisoning and the levels of contaminants found in foods.

PESTICIDE POISONING

The World Health Organisation (WHO) has estimated that between 3.5 and 5 million people globally suffer from acute pesticide poisoning every year.

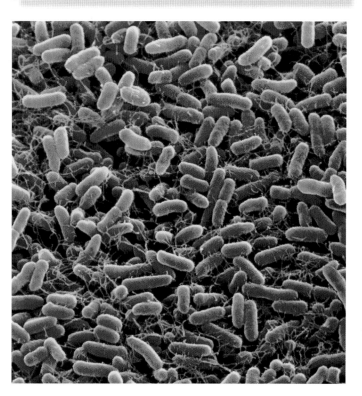

Food-borne illnesses – mainly from bacteria – are becoming increasingly common as animals are reared in close confines and given broad-scale antibiotic treatment.

A healthy diet, based around whole organic foods, is undoubtedly superior to the average Western diet, which is now linked to obesity, heart disease and a variety of other health conditions.

FOOD ADDITIVES

The Food Commission in the UK has found that consumers may be exposed to a combination of more than 60 additives in any one non-organic meal. Artificial additives are associated with a wide range of health problems, including cancer, hyperactivity, allergic reactions, mood problems, heart disease and overweight. Although all additives go through rigorous testing, in combination they may prove to be a deadly cocktail. One of the main arguments about current levels of testing is that the effects of individual substances are noted, rather than the impact of an average of 60 or more at a time. We simply do not know what these toxic chemical cocktails are doing to us.

Organic foods are free of the chemical preservatives, the many hidden sugars and unhealthy fillers, the artificial sweeteners, artificial flavourings and colourings that are currently widely used in conventional food processing. In addition, many organic foods are sugar- and salt-free, and they do not contain hydrogenated fats and oils, which have been associated with heart disease, infertility and immune-system dysfunction.

THE FACTS

◆ The Soil Association has provided evidence that organic crops contain more 'secondary metabolites' than conventionally grown plants. These form part of plants' immune systems, and also help to fight cancer in humans. The Soil Association claims that research in Denmark and Germany shows that organic crops also have a measurably higher level of vitamins, which can benefit people who eat them. By contrast, intensive farming is devitalising our food.

◆ Research carried out in 1994 by the Department of Occupational Medicine in Denmark found that men who regularly ate organic food had twice the sperm count of those on a conventional diet.

◆ In 1995 the US Environmental Working Group tested levels of pesticides in jars of babyfood: 16 different pesticides were discovered (see page 129). Children are even more vulnerable to toxins and carcinogenic (cancer-causing) substances than adults. No organic babyfood contains any pesticides.

◆ Organic produce is believed to contain higher vitamin C levels, and organic tomatoes have been found to contain 23 per cent more vitamin A than conventionally grown tomatoes. Vitamins C and A are two of the antioxidants that can prevent cancer and heart disease.

◆ Xenoestrogens ('foreign oestrogens') are oestrogen-like chemicals (oestrogens being steroid hormones responsible for female sex characteristics) from pesticides or plastics that have been linked to health problems. In the wild, some of the problems caused by them have been dramatic. For example, some fish are growing both male and female sex organs, while male alligators are becoming feminised, with hormonal levels altered to the extent that it is making reproduction difficult. The increasing levels of xenoestrogens in our environment have coincided with the earlier onset of puberty in humans, which offers a host of potential problems.

◆ In 1995 the British Ministry of Agriculture, Fisheries and Food (MAFF) issued a health warning on carrots, advising the public to peel them before eating, due to the possibility of pesticide poisoning. The US Environmental Protection Agency proved that, of several pesticides evaluated, 92 were capable of producing cancer in laboratory animals.

◆ Women with higher concentrations of certain pesticides in their bodies run a greater risk of developing breast cancer.

◆ There are 3,900 brands of insecticide, herbicide and fungicide approved for use in the UK, and some fruit and vegetables are sprayed as many as ten times before reaching supermarket shelves. In 1996 400 ton(ne)s of organophosphates were used on British crops,

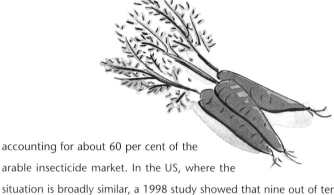

accounting for about 60 per cent of the arable insecticide market. In the US, where the situation is broadly similar, a 1998 study showed that nine out of ten children aged between six months and five years are exposed to combinations of 13 different neurotoxic organophosphate pesticides (see page 45) in their food, and one million of those children consume unsafe levels of organophosphates, which have been shown to cause long-term damage to the developing brain and nervous system.

ORGANIC FOOD AND *E. COLI*

There is an abounding myth, recently fed by a media scare, that organic produce encourages the growth of *E. coli* because organic farmers use composts and manure. Organic advocates have come out in hot defence against this claim, for the following reasons:

🐝 The levels of pathogens (substances that cause disease) in organic livestock are lower, due to high animal welfare standards and the prohibition of a reliance on antibiotics.

🐝 Standards require that manure brought on to the organic farm must be composted – a process that kills harmful bacteria.

🐝 Well-managed soils (which are the basis of organic farming) are a hive of natural biological activity, which has the ability to fight pathogens, such as unhealthy bacteria, that may come into contact with the soil. In other words, if there is bacteria present, it will soon be dealt with by healthy bacteria and beneficial insects.

🐝 Statistics from the US Center for Disease control show that the vast majority of food-borne disease is associated with cross-contamination and handling that occur later in the distribution chain and in the home, rather than on the farm.

🐝 Researchers from the University of Manitoba in Canada found that pesticides encourage dangerous bacteria, such as shigella, salmonella, *Listeria* and *E. coli* 0157:H7, to thrive on some crops.

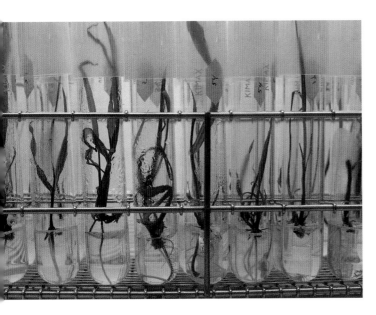

The growth and development of agricultural technology have to date produced food of inferior quality and nutritional value.

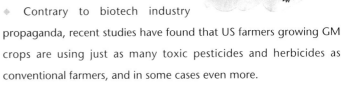

THE GM DEBATE

Genetic modification (GM; also known as genetic engineering, or GE) has health and environmental implications, and it is a process to which the organic movement is vehemently opposed. It involves isolating a gene that produces a desired characteristic. This gene is copied and then inserted into another species. The idea is that the very best qualities of plants (or even animals and humans) can be fitted together to produce the ideal product. For example, scientists have produced tomatoes that do not rot, insect-proof corn and potatoes, and other examples, the best-known genetically modified organism being the soya bean. Soya plants are particularly susceptible to herbicides, so the plan was to engineer the plants to resist only one herbicide, then to spray just that one product, leaving the weeds dead but the soya-bean plants unharmed. These soya beans are then processed into oil and flour, which are used in 60 per cent of processed foods, including cooking oils, margarines, sauces, bread, cakes, pizzas, ice creams and alternatives to dairy products.

WHY SAY NO?

◆ Contrary to biotech industry propaganda, recent studies have found that US farmers growing GM crops are using just as many toxic pesticides and herbicides as conventional farmers, and in some cases even more.

◆ 'Genetic pollution' and damage from GM field crops have already begun to cause environmental damage. Wind, rain, birds, bees and insect pollinators have begun carrying genetically altered pollen into adjoining fields, polluting the DNA of crops of both organic and non-GM farmers.

◆ The fact that GM crops are herbicide-resistant or produce their own pesticide presents dangerous problems. Pesticide-resistant pests and herbicide-resistant weeds will inevitably emerge, which means that stronger, more toxic chemicals will be required in order to deal with them.

◆ Mounting scientific evidence suggests that genetically engineered foods may present serious hazards to human health and the environment. The British Medical Association has called for a global ban on GM foods, while the *New England Journal of Medicine* has warned that 'the allergenic potential of these newly introduced microbial proteins is uncertain, unpredictable, and untestable'.

◆ An early GM amino acid is believed to have produced a powerful toxin that reportedly killed at least 37 people in the US and permanently disabled up to 1,500 others.

◆ Consumer polls over the past decade have shown that 80–95 per cent of Americans want genetically engineered foods to be labelled, in order to avoid buying them. In the EU 60 per cent of those surveyed were against GM foods.

◆ Despite new EU labelling legislation covering GM foods, most GM ingredients, such as vegetable oils, will remain unlabelled. Legislation is expected to allow up to 3 per cent GM ingredients in food as a 'tolerable' level. In the US, however, there are as yet no rulings concerning GM ingredients.

Organic food is not genetically modified.

FOOD IRRADIATION

Irradiation is a fairly new technology, which involves exposing food to high doses of radiation in order to kill the insects and pests that infest it, reduce levels of bacteria like salmonella, *E. coli* and *Listeria*, and delay ripening and rotting, so that foods can be kept for longer and can be completely sterilised. The latter is considered to be important for anyone with a weakened or immature immune system, such as the chronically or terminally ill, babies and the elderly.

In Europe consumer resistance has slowed down the introduction of irradiation. When it does occur, foods should be labelled as 'irradiated' or 'treated with ionising radiation'. But this requirement does not apply to ingredients that make up less than 25 per cent of a labelled product. The situation is, however, different in the US, where irradiation is widely used and where there have been appeals for more extensive use.

However, irradiation damages food by breaking up molecules and releasing pieces of them, known as free radicals. These damage vitamins and enzymes, and combine with existing chemicals (such as pesticides) in the food to form new ones (known as URPs), some of which are known toxins. Scientists have not studied the long-term effect of these new chemicals in our diet, so they cannot guarantee that irradiated foods are safe to eat. Irradiated foods can also lose 5–80 per cent of many vitamins (A, C, E, K and B-complex), and irradiation weakens or destroys the natural digestive enzymes found in raw foods. Organic food is not irradiated.

Genetically modified food is the subject of much controversy – here a protester pulls up genetically modified crops.

BSE AND TSE: MAD COWS AND DEER

BSE (Bovine Spongiform Encephalopathy) is a degenerative brain disease in cattle. Its origins are not entirely clear, but it is believed that its spread coincided with new feeding practices, in which the remains of cattle, and perhaps even sheep and other animals, were processed and fed to cows. CJD stands for Creutzfeldt-Jakob disease, named after the two men who discovered it. This condition is also a degenerative brain disease, and until the link with BSE was made, it was normally thought to affect elderly people. But in 1996 scientists confirmed a variant of the disease among young people, which until now they have referred to as nvCJD (new-variant CJD). It is now known as vCJD, the 'n' having been dropped because it is no longer new. There is no cure for vCJD, which causes holes in the brain and a host of physical and mental symptoms, including depression, blurred vision, slurred speech and sometimes aggressiveness, followed by loss of control over limbs and eventually of the entire body.

Cattle reared organically are entirely free of BSE, and although the cause of BSE has yet to be firmly established, there is little doubt that conventional farming practices are at its root.

The 1980s saw the biggest ever epidemic of BSE in cattle in the UK, and scientists believe that the most probable cause of vCJD in humans was the consumption of BSE-infected beef between the years 1986–9, when contaminated meat was likely to have been prevalent in the food chain. There are doubts about whether or not there will be a mass epidemic of vCJD. At least 60 people have died in the UK since 1995, but because the disease can incubate for 10–15 years it is difficult to know how many will be affected.

THE EUROPEAN PICTURE

Cases of BSE in the UK still dwarf that of any other country. But the cases are declining every year; while in several European countries the disease is on the increase.

Ireland has had 551 cases of the disease since 1989, but 104 of these were recorded in 2000 alone. Numbers of affected cattle have been steadily rising since 1996. Despite the rising numbers, Ireland has strict controls of its beef industry. Meat and bone meal are banned from cattle feed, and factories are subjected to clinical tests.

France is at the centre of the BSE fears spreading across Europe. In 1999, 153 cases of BSE were found, five times as many as the year before. Switzerland has recorded 364 cases of BSE to date, and along with Ireland and Portugal has seen one of the most rapid increases in the disease. It is also the only country in the world to test for 'hidden' BSE in the carcasses of cattle that did not show any signs of the disease prior to death. These results have prompted concerns that substantial numbers of cases are escaping detection elsewhere in Europe.

The German situation has been a source of great public indignation. Since the first outbreaks in the UK, the government repeatedly assured the public that German beef was safe. However, the discovery of the country's first two cases in 1999 shattered this illusion. Six cases were reported in 2000, and another two cases were discovered in January 2001.

What's the impact? Data from EU scientists in 1999 suggested that as many as 500,000 could die from the illness, prompting fears of a worldwide epidemic.

At present, there have been no cases of BSE in Australia or New Zealand, which claim that their beef is 'BSE-free'.

THE AMERICAN PICTURE

In the US there is concern about other transmissible spongiform encephalopathies (TSEs). Although considerably less common than BSE at the moment, chronic wasting disease (a TSE found in deer and elk) may pose a threat to those who eat infected animals. BSE-type infections have also been linked with lamb in the UK, and experts say that there are TSE diseases in sheep, mink, humans and possibly cattle and pigs. Feeding practices such as weaning calves on cattle blood protein could lead to exactly the same problems in the US as exist in the UK.

THE ORGANIC SOLUTION

Organic beef comes from the safest possible form of farming. The UK's Soil Association banned the inclusion of animal proteins in ruminant feeds in 1983, long before the emergence of the BSE crisis. There has not been a single recorded case of BSE in any herd that has been under full organic management since before 1985. The new USDA bill in the US should encourage the same safety measures.

AN ORGANIC LIFESTYLE

Adopting an organic lifestyle can improve health on all levels. Even ordinary, healthy food contains toxins that need to be broken down and excreted from the body. Our bodies are capable of consuming with relative safety potentially toxic substances that occur naturally in foods, since they are equipped with an efficient, specialised system for the elimination of toxins – our livers. Problems occur when we take in more chemicals than we can safely detoxify, or eliminate (see box).

Natural foods also contain healthy ingredients that help to counterbalance the naturally occurring chemicals. Take, for example, antioxidants, which are now known to slow down the degeneration of our bodies and to prevent cancer by inhibiting the growth of cancer-causing cells. Vitamins and minerals improve the way our bodies function, which means that everything is working at optimum levels and we deal more efficiently with chemicals in our food, among other things. And fibre helps to collect waste as it travels through our digestive system, making elimination quicker and more effective.

If your average non-organic meal contains up to 60 different toxic chemicals, your body will be put under intense pressure to eliminate them from the body. Given that there is often very little nutritional value in our food (see page 26), our bodies are not being provided with the tools they need in order to convert and remove the toxins. What happens? Toxic overload.

MORE THAN JUST FOOD

The chemicals that we use in our environments and on our bodies also increase the toxic load, and many are now known to cause health problems. Let's look at just a few examples of how ordinary, day-to-day products can cause problems:

The Western lifestyle is at the root of many health problems, including those linked to the environment. Living organically involves making choices for health and the world around us.

◆ Studies have shown that a chemical called nonylphenol – a synthetic oestrogen similar to those widely used in paints, toiletries such as skin creams, agricultural chemicals and detergents – has been linked with breast cancer. Is your moisturiser safe?

◆ Tampons may present a risk: 50 per cent of the world's cotton is now genetically modified, so unless the cotton is certified organic, then tampons could contain GM cotton. They could also contain pesticides that have been used on the cotton. These ingredients will be transmitted directly into the bloodstream. Higher-absorbency tampons also contain more rayon, which could react with bacteria to produce the toxins that cause Toxic Shock Syndrome (TSS).

◆ Scientists are investigating the link between antiperspirants and breast cancer. Dr Philippa Darbre from Reading University is investigating whether chemicals known as 'parabens', which are used as a preservative in many deodorants, might explain why more

cancers develop in a certain area of the upper breast. Both deodorants and antiperspirants can also contain aluminium, which has been linked to dementia because it has been found in patches of cell damage in the brains of people who are suffering from Alzheimer's disease.

◆ Look at the labels of the products you intend to use on or in your body: the ingredients may include petrochemical solvents, titanium dioxide (a suspected animal carcinogen), formaldehyde, pesticide residues from plant extracts, artificial sweeteners and foaming agents. Even toilet paper can be treated with dioxin-producing chlorine bleach.

TOXIC OVERLOAD

One of the body's most vital functions is to convert toxins into safe, soluble substances, which can then be eliminated in our urine, or through the gall-bladder into the intestines. The liver plays an all-important role in this detoxification process. Recent research shows that many patients with chronic fatigue syndrome or ME (myalgic encephalomyelitis) have a reduced ability to cope with toxins. In other words, their livers are not performing properly. We don't know what other disorders may be promoted by toxic overload resulting from liver dysfunction, but there is some evidence that conditions such as Parkinson's disease, motor neurone disease and Alzheimer's may be a result.

Our bodies are programmed to deal with naturally occurring toxins and, when we are healthy, they do that very well. But given that we now have serious problems with pollution, that our food is sprayed with pesticides, growth enhancers, fertilisers and then manufactured with a wide variety of other chemicals, that we drink and smoke and don't eat enough of the good foods that ensure the healthy functioning of the body – and you have a dangerous situation. Too many toxins in the body means that the liver cannot cope with the load, and that many of the toxins are not eliminated. They may be stored in fat and tissues in the body or go on to cause cell mutations or even cancer.

Consider carefully what you put on your skin. Chemicals applied topically have access to your bloodstream and, through that, to vital organs.

◆ British studies have found that the air inside our homes can be up to ten times more toxic and polluted than the air outside them.

◆ So many hazardous chemicals and substances are used in our homes on a daily basis that it is impossible to list them all, but toxic conditions are increased by the use of kitchen, bathroom and laundry cleaners, bleaches, aerosols (air fresheners, for example), polishes, paint, carpets, pet treatments, plywood, asbestos, pesticides in timber treatments and garden chemicals. (See Organic in the Home, pages 102–111.)

MAKING A CHANGE

There are now many certified organic products on the market that do not contain hazardous chemicals, which pollute our bodies and our environments. When it isn't possible to get organic, you can still make a difference by choosing products that are as natural and environmentally friendly as possible. Better still, reduce your use of personal-hygiene products altogether. Most of us have cupboards full of products that we do not really need or use. Going organic means more than simply eating organic food – why reduce your chemical intake only to overwhelm your body with other toxins?

ONE WORLD

A move towards responsible consumerism can help to support ecology and the health of our world. By making changes that increase the demand for organic products, we can help to ensure a sustainable future for our children and our children's children. Here are some of the ways in which organic living can make a difference:

🐝 You will be reducing the toxic chemicals in the environment (see pages 34–35), which can affect water supply, pollution, the food chain and even the ozone layer. Chemicals such as methyl bromide, which are regularly sprayed on conventional strawberries, are powerful ozone-eaters and are believed to be 60 times more dangerous that CFCs (chlorofluorocarbons).

🐝 By increasing the demand for organic food, you will help to encourage the health of farm workers worldwide. At present farmers are under considerable pressure to produce wide varieties and huge quantities of cheap food in order to meet demand. These intensive farming practices involve the potentially life-threatening use of chemicals, whereas organic food production does not. And if you buy 'Fair Trade' organic, you will be supporting the health and welfare of small farming communities and countries around the world. Fair Trade foods come with a guarantee that the people who produce them receive a fair price for their product and have decent working conditions.

🐝 You will be working towards a brighter future for farmers. A great deal of conventional farming is done by machine, using expensive chemicals, with the aim of producing increasingly cheap produce. The result? Farming communities throughout the Western world are facing a serious economic crisis, caused by overproduction and food scares (all of which relate to conventional farming methods). Organic farming methods not only require far more manpower, but promote good management and farming practices that will alleviate the threat of food scares and overproduction.

🐝 You will be taking steps towards reducing world hunger. According to the Soil Association, farmers' groups, charities and experts throughout the developing world believe that organic farming methods are more appropriate in developing countries, since they do not rely on 'capital-hungry' and 'debt-inducing dependency on expensive chemicals'. Organic farming focuses more heavily on domestic food requirements than on export.

🐝 And you will be doing much more than this: the benefits of organic include saving plant varieties, reducing pollution, encouraging recycling, using renewable resources, providing plants with a balanced food supply, considering the macro- and micro-ecosystems of the world and encouraging the humane treatment of people and animals everywhere.

WHY GO ORGANIC?

QUESTIONS & ANSWERS

Q How common are irradiated foods, and do they have to be labelled?

A *In Europe consumer resistance has slowed down the introduction of irradiation, but when it does occur, foods should be labelled as 'irradiated' or 'treated with ionising radiation'. However, this requirement does not apply to ingredients that make up less than 25 per cent of a labelled product. The situation is different in the US, where irradiation is widely used and where there have been appeals for more extensive use.*

Q Can pets go organic too?

A *There is a wide range of organic pet foods and other products, such as flea collars and sprays, now available. If your health-food shop or supermarket doesn't offer them, try a good mail-order company, or use natural alternatives to chemical pet treatments, such as essential oils and herbal products. Most good pet shops now offer a range of organic and natural foods and remedies for common pet ailments. Choosing organic will help to ensure your pet's future health and reduce the amount of dangerous chemicals in your home environment.*

Q My baby has allergies and drinks soya formula. Should this be organic formula?

A *There are two issues here: first, babies are much more susceptible to toxins (pesticides and other chemical residues) than adults, which makes it all the more important that they eat organically. In terms of soya, the big worry is genetic modification, which increases the need for herbicides (see page 30), among other things. There is also a concern about the production of toxins and allergies in GM foods – not a risk you want to take with your baby. Go organic: it's the only way you are assured of safety on this front.*

Q If there is no BSE in American beef, then is this the safest beef available?

A *American beef may not be known to carry BSE at present, but there are other issues. Because the market is not governed as closely as it is in the EU (in the wake of the BSE crisis), there are chances that BSE could exist either now or in the future. Furthermore, legislation in the US allows animals to be pumped full of antibiotics, growth hormones and other drugs; more chemicals are added to food, and feed can contain GM organisms; and there is a high risk of food poisoning in non-organic US beef.*

Q Can I possibly get salmonella from an organic egg?

A There is always the possibility that food-borne illnesses can be transmitted by handling, but, to date, organically farmed eggs have been shown to be free of salmonella. The reason is that the cramped, unhygienic conditions in which battery hens are raised form a breeding ground for diseases like salmonella, while organic hens are raised quite differently (see page 18), and their food does not contain any animal wastes or growth-promoting agents, or anything containing GM ingredients.

Q If only a small percentage of farms are organic, how can this way of farming be expected to feed the world?

A The idea is that countries around the world adopt organic farming methods, and that we do the same at home. The focus will then shift to producing food for domestic use, rather than selling it as cheap imports. Organic production is on the increase, and in the UK and US overall demand is growing faster than supply. Not only does this provide opportunities for growth in the home market, but there is a clear need for imports from other countries.

Q Are organic antiperspirants better than ordinary brands?

A It is actually better to avoid antiperspirants altogether, because they inhibit natural sweating, which is one of the ways in which our bodies rid themselves of toxins. I would also be surprised if you could actually find an organic antiperspirant. Your best bet is an organic deodorant, which ensures that your sweat does not smell. These are better than conventional brands, because they do not contain any chemicals that can cause health problems such as cancer (see page 35).

Q I bought some organic vegetables recently that said 'permitted pesticides used'. Aren't organic foods produced without the use of pesticides?

A If a total crop failure threatens, it is not unknown for organic farmers to use pesticides as a last resort. However, only natural pesticides will be permitted by organic certifiers, and these are strictly monitored and used under restriction. Botanical pesticides are the kind used – that is, pesticides that are derived from plants and that can be quickly broken down by sunlight.

Q If pesticides and other chemicals used in farming are so dangerous, why aren't there more deaths from them?

A The body is actually very efficient at dealing with pesticides and other chemicals and, although high levels will undoubtedly lead to death, low levels are much more insidious. Overexposure to pesticides has been linked to a wide variety of 'modern' illnesses, including infertility, chronic fatigue, allergies, irritable bowel syndrome (IBS), asthma, neurological disorders, hyperactivity and depression. Many of these are chronic conditions that affect quality of life to a serious degree.

Q If I cannot get organic, will a green cleaning product do?

A If the label says 'green' and goes on to describe why it is an environmentally friendly product, it will contain fewer damaging chemicals than conventional brands. The aim of organic living is to reduce toxic chemical consumption in any way possible, and legitimately green products can help you to do just that.

3 ORGANIC FOOD

For most people the word 'organic' instantly brings to mind food, rather than any other organic products, and much of this book is of course devoted to the subject. Organic standards are at present almost completely focused on agriculture, and the main focus of farming around the world is obviously the production of food – for both human and animal consumption.

An organic diet not only has health benefits, but the wide range of foods now available will appeal to even the most gourmet of palates.

We have seen an amazing transformation in eating habits over the past decade. The big push for convenient, processed foods is slowly but surely being replaced by consumer wariness. The reasons for this are clear – in the late 1990s there was a shift in ideology. We are no longer willing to put our health in the hands of 'experts', who have proved so fallible on so many counts. In increasing numbers we are choosing to take responsibility for our own well being, illustrated by the dramatic surge in complementary medicine, the use of nutritional supplements and the focus on preventative medicine.

Eating well is one of the cornerstones of preventative medicine, and illness has been linked – on a continuing and increasing basis – with the food we eat. We now know that conventionally farmed food often contains fewer nutrients, and that it may be weeks before it reaches our supermarket shelves, by which time what little goodness it may have contained has been even further compromised. Animal products are little better. Then there's the processing – more than two-thirds of the food that we eat in the Western world has been processed: stripped

of its nutrients (although some may be added back in), heat-treated, possibly irradiated and blended with an astonishing array of chemicals. It doesn't take a rocket scientist to work out that the majority of our food is sub-standard. It is obvious that filling our bodies with junk is going to create problems.

Bring on the food scares. Over the past decade countless legitimate problems with the food that we eat have been brought to the attention of consumers. Every single one of these problems – from salmonella and other food-poisoning agents to BSE and pesticide poisoning – has been caused by conventional, intensive farming methods. Intensive farming involves using chemicals and high technology, with the minimum amount of space for crops and livestock, to produce the greatest production levels as cheaply and quickly as possible, with no real recognition of animal welfare, renewable resources, health or the environment.

FINDING A SOLUTION

Organic food undoubtedly offers a solution. Something that is grown without the use of toxic chemicals, in soil that contains a rich source of nutrients, will always be better for us. In the long term that can have a dramatic effect on our overall health and well being. Consumers obviously agree, and Britain's biggest supermarket chain is predicting that by the year 2005 sales of its organic food will quadruple.

ORGANIC STATISTICS

Consumers are choosing organic products in ever-increasing numbers, but there are a variety of reasons for them doing so, ranging from health to environmental concerns. A survey conducted recently provided the following revealing information concerning consumers' motivations and choice of foods:

- 29 per cent of people opted to eat some organic products.
- The most popular organic product was fruit and vegetables, bought by 18 per cent of those surveyed.
- 10 per cent of people occasionally bought organic meat, dairy products and bread.
- Of those who did opt for organic alternatives, 60 per cent gave health as their main reason, while 50 per cent also said that they were attracted by the lack of pesticides.

- 46 per cent thought organic food contained more vitamins and minerals.
- 9 per cent were worried about genetic modification, and 6 per cent were concerned about the link between BSE and vCJD.
- 29 per cent thought that organic alternatives simply tasted better than traditionally farmed food.
- Only 8 per cent 'went organic' because they thought the farming practices were better for the environment.

DAIRY PRODUCTS

Dairy produce has been a subject of concern for many years, and given that it forms the basis of so much of the Western diet (in particular, that of children), it is not surprising that organic alternatives have been so successful. Although BSE has not been linked to milk, it is fairly obvious that any problems affecting cattle will make their way into milk. We know that human breastmilk can contain toxins from a mother's body, and that cows grazing in polluted areas pick up pollutants and pass them on in their milk.

Conventionally farmed dairy cows are now expected to produce up to 7,000kg/15,400lb of milk per annum, but just a hundred years ago the annual milk yield was around 1,000kg/2,200lb. To increase milk production, selective breeding has taken place and cows are separated from their calves at an early age; mastitis, ketosis, staggers and milk fever (all associated with higher milk production) have become increasingly common, requiring antibiotics to deal with them. Instead of grazing in nutrient-rich pastures, cows are now fed with high-protein foods in pellets, including various grains, soya

BOVINE SOMATOTROPIN (BST)

BST (bovine somatotropin) is a genetically engineered growth hormone that has been legally used in the US since 1994 (but has been banned by the Canadian government's health department, Health Canada, and by the EU) to increase milk production in dairy herds by up to 25 per cent. Some research claims that the hormone has been responsible for wiping out almost 20 per cent of some herds. The cows' immune systems become impaired, increasing their vulnerability to severe bladder and udder infections. It is also claimed that BST drains calcium from their bones. Many cows that survive are unable to stand, because their bones have become too weak to support them.

There are fears that the antibiotics that are used to treat cattle following BST injections could encourage the growth of antibiotic-resistant microbes that can infect humans. BST has also been linked, through high levels of a growth factor called EGF-1, to increased risks of breast, colon, muscle and prostate cancer.

beans and fish and poultry waste. These are not natural foods for plant-eating animals and can cause digestive problems, yet again requiring medication. Unless they are organically reared, dairy cows will almost certainly have eaten GM crops in their feed.

THE ORGANIC ALTERNATIVE

Organically raised cows graze on organic pastures that have not been treated with any pesticides or fertilisers, which means that fewer (if any) residues exist in their milk. The health of the animals is encouraged, with homeopathy or herbalism often being the first line of treatment when an animal does become ill. Pastures contain nutrient-rich and varied grasses and plants. Organic dairy cows cannot be kept indoors or permanently tethered, and are less likely to suffer from the health problems associated with unhygienic, cramped conditions. The yield of an organic dairy cow is much lower than that of a conventionally raised dairy cow, but no stimulants, such as BST, can be used.

Organic milk and dairy products are free of chemical residues that may be harmful to health. Also important, however, is the fact that organic dairy cows are reared humanely.

ORGANIC DAIRY PRODUCTS

◆ SOUR CREAM, CRÈME FRAÎCHE AND CREAM: organic options contain no GM ingredients and use only organic milk. Lecithin, which is often genetically modified, is frequently used in UHT and reduced-fat/low-calorie brands of conventional cheese.

◆ ICE CREAM: organic brands contain no GM ingredients and cannot use BST milk. Only 5 per cent of the ingredients can be non-organic, but these must be GM-free.

◆ YOGHURT: organic yoghurts should be free of both artificial flavourings and additives. As with some other products, they may use up to 5 per cent non-organic ingredients, but these must be GM-free and fully traceable. Only organic milk can be used to make organic yoghurt.

◆ ORGANIC CHEESE: uses non-GM vegetarian rennet. No colourings, except for annatto (a naturally red colouring traditionally used to make Red Leicester and Double Gloucester cheese), are used. Organic cheese uses only certified organic milk.

With the growth of organic agriculture, less common varieties are being produced again, providing a veritable cornucopia of healthy offerings.

THE ISSUES

◆ Environmental group Friends of the Earth claims that some apples are sprayed with pesticides up to 35 times before they reach the shops. Some 50 different chemicals are used on apples alone.

◆ The UK's Pesticides Residue Committee (PRC) found pesticide residues in 27 per cent of food tested – of these, 2 per cent contained levels above the legal limits.

◆ Conventionally grown bananas use enormous quantities of pesticides, including organophosphates (see box).

ORGANIC FRUIT AND VEGETABLES

The main issue affecting conventionally farmed fruit and vegetables is the use of pesticides, which has been linked to a wide variety of health problems (see pages 28–29 and page 39). Researchers claim that the most heavily sprayed foods include lettuces, oranges, pears, apples, celery and carrots. However, GM fresh tomatoes and GM potatoes that are designed to provide a higher starch content are already available in the US, and other fruit and vegetables are likely to follow in the near future. There is growing concern in the Western world that many of the fruit and vegetables we buy have now been cross-pollinated by GM crops.

◆ The US Consumers' Union found that many fruit and vegetables carry pesticide residues that exceed the limits which the EPA (Environmental Protection Agency) considers safe for children. According to the Consumers' Union Report, even one serving of some fruit and vegetables can exceed the safe daily limits for young children.

◆ Methyl parathion (an organophosphate) accounts for most of the total toxicity of the foods that were analysed, particularly peaches, frozen and canned green beans, pears and apples.

◆ A pesticide called chlormequat is used to improve the yield and shape of pears. It has never been licensed for use in the UK – and yet in 1999 pears sold and eaten in Britain were found to contain up to five times more pesticide than the legal limit.

◆ The EPA considers 60 per cent of all herbicides, 90 per cent of all fungicides and 30 per cent of all insecticides to be potentially carcinogenic (cancer-causing).

◆ Future fruit and vegetables are likely to be genetically modified so that they freeze and defrost well.

◆ Mushrooms are normally grown in compost made from manure from animals fed on a proportion of GM feed. Non-organic mushroom growers use chemical pesticides and formaldehyde, as well as methyl bromide (see page 37) and fungicides.

◆ Almost all non-organic corn is genetically modified.

◆ In tests carrots are regularly found to exceed maximum residue levels (MRLs). They are often treated with organophosphates.

CHOOSING ORGANIC

◆ Organic fruit and vegetables can be purchased in many forms, including fresh, dried, tinned and frozen. They will not contain chemical pesticides.

◆ They are always grown in organic soil.

◆ Don't be surprised to find that your organic products go off more quickly. No preservatives, waxes, irradiation or genetic engineering are used to extend their shelf life.

◆ Organic fruit and vegetables may be oddly shaped and less colourful than non-organic. Don't be put off – this is the natural appearance, as nature intended.

◆ These foods are more nutritious, taste much better and often contain more fibre.

◆ Organic fruit and vegetables are often pre-packaged to ensure that they are indeed organic. If you buy them loose, ask to see some evidence of certification.

ORGANOPHOSPHATES (OPS)

Organophosphates are one of the most worrying types of pesticides currently being used. They are neurological poisons and work on humans in much the same way as they do on insects. Some of their effects include damage to the nervous system, causing headaches, blurred vision, difficulty in breathing, vomiting and loss of memory. Later, convulsions, coma and even death can result. In the UK the Pesticide Action Network UK believes that these chemicals – which are widely used on apples, bananas, carrots, cabbages, broccoli, mushrooms, soft fruit and potatoes – should be banned. In the US the EPA is re-evaluating organophosphates. Since its review began in 1996 the agency has removed from the market five of the 43 pesticides in that group.

45

An apple a day? Unless it's organic, you could be eating something that has been sprayed up to 40 times with over 100 chemicals.

Organic apples are not only healthier, but the fruit and its juice taste infinitely better than commercially grown brands.

DRINKING ORGANIC

In health terms, what you drink is just as important as what you eat. Fortunately, in addition to organic food, there is an ever-increasing variety of organic drinks on the market to appeal to all ages and tastes. Choosing organic drinks means that you are naturally reducing the number of chemicals involved in their manufacture. Organic fruit and vegetable juices are prepared from organic produce, and all of the benefits of these products will be present in your choice of drink.

Remember, however, that it is important to choose 'healthy' organic drinks over those that have little or no nutritional value. For example, organic cola is preferable to non-organic, in that natural flavours and sweeteners are used; however cola is not in itself a healthy drink. The word 'organic' does not necessarily mean 'good for you' (see page 126), and consumers are frequently being hoodwinked into choosing organic products over conventional brands in place of healthy alternatives.

SOME OF THE MAIN CONSIDERATIONS

◆ For health, the best options are organic fruit and vegetable juices. These are grown without pesticides and other toxic chemicals, and even the packaging has to meet organic specifications. Freshly squeezed juices should be your first choice, but concentrates are fine.
◆ There is controversy over whether water can be certified organic. There are 'organic' brands, but critics claim that there is no way that they can reasonably trace the source of underground springs.

◆ Organic squashes are produced without the use of citric acid and artificial sweeteners, such as aspartame. But even organic brands can contain high levels of sugar (natural though these are), so all squashes should be heavily diluted with pure water.

ALCOHOLIC DRINKS

Organic beer, wine and spirits are a much better bet than non-organic alternatives. The hops that are used for making beer are generally grown with nitrates, organophosphates (see page 45), herbicides and fungicides. GM yeasts are also approved for use, and GM strains of barley are currently under development. Organic hops, however, are grown without any of these. The biggest manufacturers of organic beer are the Germans, who produce a higher yield of organic hops.

Organic spirits are now available and do not contain any GM ingredients or chemical flavourings and colourings.

Wine is not at present affected by the GM revolution, although research into GM wine is under way in the US, Australia and France. GM yeasts are approved for use, but are not widely utilised at present. However, sulphur dioxide (a preservative) is heavily used in non-organic wines, and vineyards are sprayed with a cocktail of chemicals, including fertilisers, pesticides and fungicides. Many non-organic wines contain traces of these chemicals. Organic grapes are grown according to strict organic standards, and are, it appears, less likely to cause hangovers!

Organic carbonated soft drinks are claimed to be of a much higher quality than conventional brands. Normally filtered mineral water is used, along with organic juices, cane juices and natural flavourings. But beware of replacing healthier drinks with what are effectively junk drinks. If you want a soft drink as a treat, choose organic.

TEA, COFFEE AND HOT CHOCOLATE

IFOAM (see page 16) has set out key requirements for producing these drinks, and they include the following:

• Natural fermentation processes must be used.

• Crops should be free of all residue and samples tested regularly.

• Crops should be produced as part of a sustainable farming system and the entire farm must be organic.

The overuse of chemicals is a real problem in coffee production, because many of the countries producing the beans are not subject to the same bans on highly toxic chemicals as the US and the EU.

Similarly, quality control is not necessarily as strict; pesticides, fungicides, and treatments to prevent rust are widely used.

Black tea has traditionally been produced with expensive and toxic chemicals, which have caused soil erosion and river pollution. Increasingly tea producers are changing to organic farming methods, which have proved to be less expensive and more productive. However, unless a product says 'organic', it won't comply with all the restrictions that govern organic agriculture and it may contain traces of chemicals. Much the same holds true for green tea, although, because of its health-giving properties, the majority of green teas now available are certified organic. Herbal teas can be heavily sprayed during growing and production, and GM ingredients may be used in flavourings. Stick to organic brands if you can.

ORGANIC FISH

Fish can be organic, and this has both health and environmental impacts. Fishing has been affected by the need to supply high quantities at cheaper prices. Farmed fish have become increasingly common, which has raised a number of issues.

First, farmed fish are likely to have been given food containing GM ingredients and are more susceptible to disease, because large concentrations of fish are kept in one place, normally in underwater cages. The answer? Antibiotics – and plenty of them – are fed to the fish *en masse*. These are not only passed on to the consumer, but infiltrate the water supply, which could lead to antibiotic resistance in humans. Conditions also demand the use of fungicides, algaecides, organophosphates and copper-based anti-foulants.

Farmed fish are fed on a diet that often contains recycled dead fish, fish oils and colourings. The food is padded out with bran and a variety of chemicals, including hormones. These have environmental implications. When farmed fish enter the wild, they can spread disease, parasites and genes, reducing biodiversity and the fertility of fish (due to the growth hormones). According to new research, farmed salmon can contain up to ten times the amounts of pollutants found in wild salmon. Furthermore, even wild fish absorb high levels of environmental pollutions. Studies show that cod and other sea fish have high levels of pesticide and other residues stored in their bodies. While these toxins may fall below MRLs, the long-term effect of fat-soluble chemicals on the body is unknown.

THE NEW ORGANIC STANDARDS

The Soil Association in the UK will be issuing a kite-mark for organic fish in the near future, and already there is a movement towards meeting new standards. Criteria have been drawn up for organic fish farming, to include breeding, environmental impact, animal welfare, water source and quality, the treatment of disease, harvesting and feed: fish farmers cannot feed fishmeal from industrial fishing, artificial or synthetic colourings, growth regulators, hormones or appetite stimulants, or anything derived from GM foods. Certified organic fish is now available, and it tastes infinitely superior.

Conventionally farmed fish are awash with disease that requires chemical treatment, and both disease and chemicals can spread to the environment. Also, fish feed can be genetically modified and contain chemicals that are harmful to human health.

GRAINS, BREADS AND BAKED GOODS

Conventionally farmed grains are heavily sprayed with toxic chemicals, and because the grains are very small, they are able to absorb more pesticides than other foods. In addition, bakery products and pastas (indeed, anything that has been made with flour) can be 'improved' with soya flour, which may well be genetically modified. Most baked goods include a host of additives and chemicals to improve their shelf life, keep the bread soft, bleach the flour, increase the volume of the dough and provide colour and flavouring. What is more, like most things on our supermarket shelves, flour-based products have often been heavily refined, which means that important nutrients have been lost.

Organic breads and grains are a sensible alternative, given the pesticide issue. All organic bread, for example, must contain at least 95 per cent organic ingredients. GM yeasts and other GM ingredients are not permitted. The same goes for organic baked goods and pastas, and even for organic cereals.

However, remember the health issues: a refined white organic roll will not be healthier than a non-organic wholemeal roll. Undoubtedly fewer chemicals will be involved in the growing and processing of ingredients, but refined foods contain little fibre or other nutrients. The best options are always wholemeal or wholegrain breads, rolls, cereals and pastas – and, wherever possible, organic is your best bet.

Similarly, organic cakes will be superior to non-organic alternatives, but they should only be eaten in moderation, for obvious health reasons. Once again, go for organic cakes and biscuits that contain sultanas, raisins, honey, nuts and other 'healthy' organic ingredients over those that have been heavily refined and sweetened.

Wholegrains are one area where it's important to go organic. Pesticides and other chemicals sit on the husk of the grain, which forms part of wholewheat breads and other products. So, paradoxically, a refined white non-organic bread will be less tainted than its wholemeal equivalent, although certainly lower in nutrients.

ORGANIC MEAT

The demand for meat around the world has led to a type of factory farming with appalling animal welfare standards together with a preponderance of toxic chemicals, which can affect anything from immune function to fertility in humans. Here we focus on two of the main concerns surrounding meat and poultry production: antibiotics and growth hormones.

ANTIBIOTICS

◆ Pigs are given up to ten different antibiotics to promote growth and prevent the many diseases to which they are vulnerable when kept in close confinement and under stress.

◆ Chickens are routinely fed growth-promoting antibiotics, which are used to treat parasitic infections. Treatment is given to all of them, whether necessary or not.

◆ Eggs present a real problem: antibiotic residues have been found in up to 10 per cent of eggs. Intensive free-range birds and those living in perchery systems are often routinely given growth-promoting antibiotics to control necrotic enteritis.

◆ In the UK intensively reared cattle are permitted several growth-promoting antibiotics in their feed. In the US 22.7 million kg/50 million lb of antibiotics are produced each year; 9 million kg/20 million lb are given to animals, of which 80 per

Conventionally reared pigs are taken from their mothers soon after birth, and given hormones and antibiotics as part of their feed. Organic pigs must to be raised non-intensively, with access to healthy feed, exercise, fresh air and daylight.

cent is used on livestock merely to promote more rapid growth. The remaining 20 per cent is used to help control the diseases that occur under such confined conditions.

WHY DOES IT MATTER?

The Soil Association believes that increasing resistance to antibiotics presents a serious threat to human health, and that it could be infinitely greater and more costly than BSE (see pages 32–33). Studies show that we are facing a major epidemic of diseases that have developed multiple drug resistance. At least four of these (strains of salmonella, *E. coli*, campylobacter and enterococci) arise directly as a result of the overuse of antibiotics in agriculture.

WHY ORGANIC?

- Organic sheep and lamb farmers do not use the organophosphates commonly added to sheep dip, which has health and environmental implications.
- Apart from the fact that no antibiotics or growth promoters are given to organic pigs, there are no fillers or added water in organic hams and bacon.
- Organic fowl does not contain extra water (injected into the carcass), and the routine use of antibiotics is prohibited.
- No GM products are used in the feed of organic animals.
- No antibiotics or growth promoters are permitted to be used in organic farming.
- BSE has never been found in an organic cow.
- Organic meat tastes considerably better.

Recent scientific research has confirmed that antibiotics, routinely fed to factory farm animals to make them grow faster, are creating dangerous antibiotic-resistant pathogens that are infecting people who eat these animal products. Chickens are reservoirs for many food-borne pathogens, including campylobacter and salmonella. In the EU 75 per cent of chickens contain salmonella and in the US 20 per cent of broiler chickens are contaminated in the processing plant with salmonella and 80 per cent with campylobacter. The latter pathogen is the most common known cause of bacterial food-borne illness in the US.

GROWTH HORMONES

In the US at least one in six farmers injects his cows with genetically engineered growth hormone to promote weight gain. Around 90 per cent of the 13 billion kg/29 billion lb of beef consumed by Americans each year comes from cattle that have been fattened by hormone implants. For pork, the figure is almost 100 per cent. The EU has, for this reason, banned American beef from its shelves.

Why the concern? The EU's Scientific Committee has highlighted that one of the hormones used is a known carcinogen, and has listed many other potential health risks.

There are also issues involving human hormone activity. In the US six 'natural' sex hormones are given to animals to increase their weight by as much as 23kg/50lb and are obviously present in the meat itself. According to some estimates, an eight-year-old boy who ate two hamburgers made from this meat would, following the meal, have increased his levels of female sex hormones by 10 per cent.

ORGANIC FOOD

10

QUESTIONS

& ANSWERS

Q Why does organic meat look fattier than non-organic?

A *Organic meat looks as meat should look – it has a healthy marbled appearance. The feed used by conventional farmers is designed to prevent fat by increasing lean muscle tissue. This is often done with the aid of growth-promoting hormones (see page 51), which are decidedly unhealthy. Good-quality beef, for example, should have a nice marbling of creamy white fat (yellow if the cow is fed on grass), which makes it more succulent, tender and tasty when cooked.*

Q The yolks of my organic eggs are not very yellow. Does this mean they are of poorer quality?

A *Organic eggs are likely to be less vivid in colour, particularly during the winter, because the hens are not given feed that contains yellow colouring (astaxanthin or castaxanthin) to enrich the appearance of the yolk. They are of a superior quality to non-organic brands.*

Q Are free-range chickens an alternative to organic?

A *Not really. Free-range chickens can still be given feed containing GM ingredients, which is only one issue here. Strictly speaking, 'free-range' means nothing more than the fact that the birds have daytime access to open-air runs for at least half their lives, and during the final fattening stage 70 per cent of the birds' diet must be cereal. There are no legal restrictions on the inclusion of growth-promoting medication, and the chickens are still kept in huge, industrial-sized flocks.*

Q How do I know that the meat I am eating does not contain growth hormones?

A *Unless you eat only organic, you cannot be sure. Although there is a ban in the EU on using hormones to encourage growth in animals, there is evidence that they are used on many conventional farms. In the US growth hormones can be used legally – and are.*

Q Is wild fish better than organic?

A First of all, there is no legal obligation for retailers to state whether a fish is farmed or wild, and you can assume that it's farmed unless the label says otherwise. Wild fish is expensive, but there is no evidence to show that it contains toxic residues that could harm human health. The further out the fish is caught, the better the chances that it is free of contaminants. Genuinely wild fish is, therefore, an alternative to organic farmed fish, but organic is much better than conventionally farmed fish.

Q Are frozen organic vegetables as healthy as fresh?

A Vegetables are frozen as soon as they are picked, so they are normally high in vitamins and minerals, particularly vitamin C, which begins to be lost from fresh foods once they are removed from the plant. However, because organic food spoils more quickly than conventionally grown food (see page 45), you can be sure that the varieties you get in markets or on the supermarket shelves are fresh, which means that they should be nutritious. Frozen vegetables are a good second best if you cannot get fresh.

Q I have heard that fish oils are added to the diet of farmed fish. Isn't this a good thing, given their health benefits?

A Adding fish oils to fish food may increase the amount of oil in fish such as salmon, but any positive effects are diminished by the conditions in which the fish are raised. Furthermore, toxins are stored in fat, so there is a double whammy: there are more toxins and more fat in these fish, so you will be getting twice the level of contamination. Choose organic.

Q Are organic calves raised for veal more humanely treated?

A Calves that are reared for organic veal are encouraged to suckle throughout their lives, and they enjoy much better welfare conditions. You can expect the meat to be pinker and firmer, with a stronger flavour. This is largely because they have been given the opportunity to roam outdoors, rather than being shut in blackened sheds to encourage the production of white meat.

Q Are tinned organic vegetables a healthier option?

A All tinning processes (organic included) reduce the level of beneficial nutrients. However, organic brands are superior to non-organic, because the vegetables are free of pesticides and other nasties (see pages 28–29 and page 129), and they do not contain colourings, which may be genetically modified. And no organic foods can be GM, which has obvious health implications.

Q If organic biscuits and cakes are just as unhealthy as non-organic brands, why choose them?

A The first reason is because they are free of GM ingredients, which appear in almost all conventionally manufactured goodies. Second, no unnatural or toxic chemicals are used in either the growing or the baking process, which means that you will, at the very least, be cutting down on your toxic load.

4 BUYING ORGANIC

The decision to 'go organic' involves paying much closer attention to the labels on foods and other products that you buy and necessarily involves a certain amount of detective work! While organic products are now much more widely available than they were in the past, you may have to look further afield for alternatives to the conventional foods and products that you are accustomed to using. That is where the fun begins.

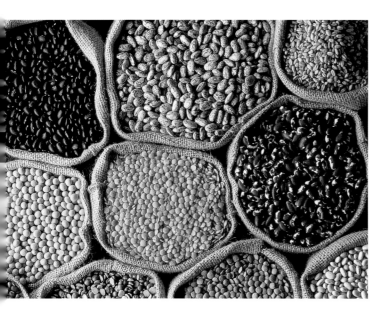

First, you need to familiarise yourself with the various kite-marks and logos that prove that a product is organic. It is easy to be tricked by 'lookalike' and 'soundalike' images and selling lines, but if a product is genuinely organic, then a reputable certification body will say so on the label.

One of the greatest pleasures of choosing organic food is the fact that you will be encouraged to try new varieties. Farmers' markets and box schemes (see pages 58–59 and 60) are based around local produce, which means that you will end up trying vegetables that you may never have

Watch out for certified organic kite-marks, which vary between countries.

The wide variety of organic foods that are available at farmers' markets can tempt any palate, and encourage experimentation with the less common varieties. Most farmers are normally pleased to provide customers with advice on cooking and recipes.

seen before. There is also a certain satisfaction to be gained from choosing products that will benefit the environment and rural communities. When you buy direct from farmers, or support small industry through mail-order schemes, you will be helping to support an economy that has altruistic aims (see page 37).

ORGANIC SOURCES

The range and diversity of organic products are increasing on an almost daily basis, but one of the best ways to find what you are looking for is to locate a good local health-food shop that carries organic products. You should be able to find one that stocks both organic foods and cleaning products, as well as health and beauty items. The staff of smaller outlets are more likely to be involved in the purchase and sale of the products and will, therefore, have an interest in and knowledge of all things organic. If you need advice, this is a good first-stop. Organic farmers' markets are another great source of food products. Some of those in the US and UK are open to the public, and you can learn a lot about organic farming methods – and even take part – while purchasing the foods you need.

Literally hundreds of mail-order companies, websites and delivery services have now been set up to sell and deliver organic products, so if time is at a premium you don't have to spend a whole day choosing your goods. Supermarkets have also increased their lines of organics, and you can get almost everything you need through normal channels, as long as you are prepared to take the time to choose carefully, reading the labels.

TIPS ON BUYING ORGANIC

🐝 Choose a good independent health-food, wholefood or organic shop as your first port of call.

🐝 Check your local telephone directory for details of farmers' markets in your area. Some run only biweekly or even monthly, so you will need to establish their frequency.

🐝 If you don't find what you want on your supermarket shelves, order it. Most supermarkets are prepared to stock an item that they know will sell – even if only to you.

🐝 Don't hesitate to ask suppliers whether they can provide you with other products. Many organic delivery services and mail-order companies do not list all the products that they can supply, or may be able to order in something special.

🐝 Buy a good organic directory. In the UK, the best one is published by the Soil Association (see pages 136 and 138). In Australia and New Zealand, specific organic directories are also available.

🐝 Don't hesitate to ask for proof of organic certification. By law companies and even farmers must be able to provide this. If they can't, don't buy from them.

🐝 If you are unsure about using new organic products, see if you can get them in trial sizes, to ensure that they meet your needs.

Organic produce is flown in from all over the world, and many small plantations and farms are finding that organic farming is not only safer for their workers, but more economical.

THE ORGANIC SUPERMARKET

Organics are big business, and supermarket chains have been quick to jump on the bandwagon. They do offer obvious advantages. First, they can buy in bulk, which brings down the price of some goods. They are also able to import organic products from around the world, which means that you can simply replace non-organic kiwis, for example, with those that meet organic standards. It can be a difficult transition for consumers to start using completely local produce if they are accustomed to enjoying foods from around the world. And the growth of the all-organic supermarket has meant that you can shop in these outlets with complete confidence. Some of the bigger chains now also sell clothing, paint, gardening products and even carpets.

However, there are drawbacks: the benefits to the environment of organic farming are obviously seriously undermined if the products are then flown halfway around the world, using up petrol and creating pollution. Furthermore, if you can always get organic Golden Delicious apples flown in from abroad, you are much less likely to try the lesser-known varieties grown locally.

IS MY FOOD FRESH?

Organic goods ripen and therefore rot more quickly than non-organic foodstuffs (due to a lack of preservatives, irradiation and other such factors). It is important, therefore, that you know what to look out for when purchasing fresh foods:

Fruit and vegetables should be firm and have a fresh, rather than overly sweet or cloying, scent. Foods such as broccoli, cucumbers and celery should not be rubbery.

Organic salad leaves are often heartier than non-organic brands and should be crisp. Don't worry about insects or any slight browning on the edges. If the majority of the plant is firm, it is likely to be fresh.

Root vegetables should be firm, with an unbroken skin.

Frozen foods should be at freezing temperature, and kept that way, to maintain their freshness and avoid contamination. Choose packages from the bottom of the freezer, and save your freezer shopping until last, so that you have the chance to get them home before they defrost.

Open egg cartons before you buy them, to check that the eggs are not dirty. Cracked eggs are open to infection. If there is any 'fur' on the eggs, they may be mouldy.

Organic cheeses look much like non-organic brands, although they may be less highly coloured. Hard cheese should look firm, without any trace of mould (except in blue cheeses of course). Soft cheese in crusts should fit their shells neatly and should show no signs of leaking.

Organic butter is less highly coloured than non-organic.

Organic bread should have a firm crust, without any signs of peeling. Wholemeal crusts should be dark brown. The loaf should be fairly heavy if it contains the right amount of air.

Raw meat should look firm, fresh and a healthy pink colour. Anything greying or bleached is not recommended for eating. Remember that organic produce is often less brightly coloured than non-organic.

Organic lamb should be a rich pink and nicely marbled. Winter lamb will be a darker red.

Organic beef should be a dark, purplish-red, with white or yellow fat marbled throughout. Organic veal is darker than non-organic, because the calves are treated more humanely.

Organic pork should be pale pink with a slight sheen. It should not look flaccid or greasy.

When choosing fish, don't buy anything that smells strongly. Look for clear eyes, red gills, shiny skin and scales in place. The fish should feel firm and slightly resilient if you press it. Avoid fish with dull eyes or slimy skin. Organic fish such as rainbow trout and salmon will be less pink than their non-organic counterparts.

Most importantly, keep your eye on the 'sell-by' dates. Organic foods do not contain chemical preservatives and are more likely to 'go off' quickly. If you cannot eat the food as soon as it is purchased, freeze it (if it is freezer-safe) until you are ready to enjoy it.

FARMERS' MARKETS

Farmers' markets are springing up all over the US, Europe and the UK, partly in response to the demand for fresh food and partly because they offer undoubted health benefits. Buying direct from a farmer means that you know exactly where the food comes from and that it is more likely to be fresh – often picked the same day.

The farmers' market is a cornucopia of shops in one: a greengrocer, butcher, baker, deli, florist, fishmonger and garden centre. Along with fruit, vegetables and salads, farmers often sell lamb, beef, pork, chicken, venison, cheese, eggs, mushrooms, honey, wine, juice, jams, jellies, chutneys, baked goods, plants, cut flowers and herbs. There may be home-made meat pies, quiches, smoked chicken and fish, flavoured sausages and pâtés; native foods, as well as locally grown imports; traditional, or heritage, varieties of fruit and vegetables; and the meat of rare-breed animals. There may also be unusual offerings, such as striped beetroots, golden courgettes, giant ostrich eggs, unfiltered honey and bee pollen.

Organic farmers' markets are carefully monitored to ensure that all of the goods being sold are indeed organic, but ordinary farmers' markets can be just as good – if a farmer is selling at local markets, he or she is less likely to be using the conventional, intensive farming methods that are necessary to produce huge crops at cheap prices. You may find that many of the farmers at your local market use organic methods, in that they allow their animals to roam freely, give them chemical-free feed and avoid the use of growth hormones and other drugs. Before organic became a fashionable term and a legal definition, many farmers ran chemical-free, natural farms. Many still do. So if you cannot find organic produce locally, try a farmers' market. Talk to the farmers, before buying, about how their food is produced. If they cannot provide organic certification, they can usually speak knowledgeably about how it was grown.

Visiting a farmers' market is one way of supporting sustainable local food economies, which provide more local jobs and reduce pollution. At present, the global economy is unsustainable. Do your part!

CHOOSING YOUR FOOD

◆ Bear in mind the qualities that fresh food should have (see page 57), and if something looks or feels different from what you would expect, then ask why. Use your nose! Fresh organic food has a strong but pleasant scent. It does not smell overly sweet or perfumed. If something doesn't smell good, don't buy it.

◆ Remember organic anomalies: when grown naturally, organic fruit and vegetables will be oddly shaped and perhaps even blemished. As long as it smells fresh, is firm to the touch and has an unbroken skin, it will be fine.

◆ Most farmers will allow – and even encourage – you to taste their various offerings. Be adventurous, and go for foods you might not normally buy.

◆ Organic farmers normally exhibit evidence of organic certification, particularly for goods that are not pre-packaged (such as cheeses, wines and honey). If they don't do so, then you are perfectly entitled to ask to see it. Remember that something like bread must have 95 per cent or more of its ingredients coming from organic sources. If there is no symbol (see page 16 and pages 116–118) on the packaging, the seller must be able to show evidence of the source of all ingredients. That may sound like splitting hairs, but organic standards are crucial to the success of the industry and to making a wide-ranging change in the way that food is produced. If they are being broken, or if consumers are being misled in any way, this obviously undermines the hard work and effort of all organic farmers and organisations.

Be prepared to find a wide variety of different foods at an organic farmers' market, all of which will be grown to strict organic standards; some may even have been picked that day.

59

ORGANIC IN THE COMMUNITY

One of the drawbacks of our convenience-orientated society is that we expect to be able to find what we want quickly and effortlessly. In the past organic growers and manufacturers had to struggle to meet these demands, but things have changed dramatically over the last few years and organic producers have now found ways to give consumers what they want: box-delivery schemes, good local selection, mail-order and even Internet facilities with home deliveries.

From an organic point of view, the community-based schemes are the most valued. They tend to be organised by small farmers and rural companies, providing produce to local areas and shops. This encourages the growth of the local rural community at grassroots level, and helps keep it alive.

BOX SCHEMES

Once hard to come by, these small (but growing) businesses cater to local communities by delivering organic goods to the home on a regular basis. You can either choose what and how much you want in advance, or leave it to the delivery service to choose the freshest seasonal goods, based on the quantity you require (from a one-person box to a family-sized one). Both ways of using the schemes are good ones. Some consumers are unlikely to use the more obscure produce that makes its way into the boxes, and will benefit more from a regular order of the same items. However, choosing a box selected by the delivery service can be a delight, with a treasure trove of unusual goodies. Contact the Soil Association in the UK or Organic Consumers' Association in the US for details of schemes.

Small farmholdings in your neighbourhood are likely to provide most of the products that are packed in local box schemes and sold in nearby shops, so you will benefit your own community by using such sources.

POINTS TO REMEMBER

◆ Many box schemes now deliver wines, juices, cleaning agents and even organic clothing as a secondary line, so if you don't see what you want listed, don't be afraid to ask.

◆ Make sure that you check the prices of goods before you order. Some companies include delivery in their prices, while others charge extra for this service. It is always best to be aware of the final bill in advance.

◆ Alternatively, many schemes allow you to set a price and then choose items to suit your budget. This may mean having more seasonal produce than home-grown imports, but is one way of keeping the costs down.

◆ Nationwide organic delivery services tend to be slightly more expensive than local schemes, but you may find that they offer you more variety.

◆ Local schemes use local farmers, so if one of your reasons for shopping organic is to help small farmholdings in your area, then this is your best bet.

◆ Don't be afraid to send back sub-standard goods. Even the best-run delivery schemes can make a mistake from time to time by underestimating the ripening time of fruit, for example. The food you receive should be of good quality and very fresh (see page 57). If it is not, ask for a replacement.

◆ Make sure you set up convenient delivery times. It can be frustrating to depend upon delivery schemes for the bulk of your shopping, only to find that this has been delayed. Confirm times in advance and, if your service is continually late, then consider using another service.

◆ Ask to try some of the different products on offer. Most delivery services are keen to encourage customers to buy more and will gladly put in some 'extras' to tempt you.

◆ Don't hesitate to ask suppliers for proof of organic certification. Most box schemes and other delivery services provide unpackaged goods. The company's literature should show evidence of certification; if it doesn't, then they should be able to produce it.

LOCAL SHOPS

The number of local shops selling organic produce is on the increase, and many good health-food and wholefood shops are now catering to the new demand. As discussed on page 55, these shops can be a mine of information for newly organic customers, and they can often order products that you will not find in delivery schemes or on supermarket shelves. Once again, evidence of organic certification should be available on request.

Many shops allow you to order organic produce (and other fresh products, such as bread or meat) for later collection or even delivery to your door. Ask about the different options that are available from them – or you can even try suggesting that they start a new service. Local shops are much more likely to offer fresh produce, normally collected or delivered from the farm or a farmers' market that day, and they will generally provide you with a greater variety of produce than the average supermarket. Supporting your local shop will help to keep small businesses and, through them, small farms alive.

ORGANIC EVERYTHING?

There are limitations on what can be labelled organic at present, but these are now being addressed by international and national standards boards. Manufacturers keen to leap on the 'organic' bandwagon may find areas of the market that are largely unregulated and take advantage of consumer ignorance to make big money. The answer is to look for organic kite-marks or certification on anything you buy that claims to be organic.

It's now possible to make your environment almost completely organic. Feed your baby a healthy organic dinner and then pop her into bed between crisp, organically produced cotton sheets.

WHAT IS AVAILABLE ON THE ORGANIC MARKET?

The following organic products can be purchased through local shops, mail-order schemes, the Internet, delivery services or at farmers' markets:

- baby foods
- baby formulas
- bedding
- body-care products
- children's paint
- clothing
- confectionery
- cosmetics
- fabrics
- feminine protection
- floor polish
- furniture polish
- gardening supplies
- herbal products
- household glue
- laundry detergents
- nappies
- natural remedies
- nutritional supplements
- paints
- pet foods
- seeds
- soaps
- sunscreens
- toiletries
- toothpaste
- towels and bed linen
- toys
- wallpaper adhesive
- wood preservatives

WHAT IF YOU CAN'T FIND ORGANIC?

The next best bet is a legitimately 'green' or eco-friendly product. If you aren't sure what to use, contact a reputable mail-order company or visit an all-organic supermarket. For example, Planet Organic in the UK has a policy of not stocking anything processed using artificial ingredients and all their products are organic, as far as possible. Cleaning products can be a bit more troublesome. You want to avoid products that contain any of these:

◆ PHOSPHATES: these are used as water softeners and to improve cleaning in dishwasher detergents and washing powders. They stimulate the growth of algae in receiving waters, which in turn starve the water of oxygen, killing fish and plant life.

◆ ENZYMES: these can cause severe skin irritations and asthma. They can be genetically engineered.

◆ CHLORINE BLEACHES (in conventional toilet cleaners, washing powders and dishwasher detergents): when broken down, these create carcinogenic, toxic substances.

◆ EDTA (ethylenediamine tetra-acetic acid): this is used in cleaning products as a substitute or in addition to phosphates. It attracts heavy metals, such as lead and mercury, which have carcinogenic properties. These can find their way into water supplies and be very difficult to remove.

◆ OPTICAL BRIGHTENERS: these are used in washing powders to give the illusion of 'whiteness' by attaching themselves to fabrics to reflect white light. They are difficult to biodegrade and can cause severe skin irritation. They also cause mutations to marine life in receiving waters.

◆ PETROLEUM-BASED ADDITIVES: present in most household cleaners, these often incompletely break down and contain toxic impurities, which can cause allergic reactions and endanger plant and animal life.

BODY-CARE PRODUCTS

Products for use on the body should be free from harsh foaming agents, petrochemicals, artificial perfumes, colourants, animal ingredients and unnecessary synthetic additives. Organic ingredients should be included wherever possible (for example, organic essential oils for their antibacterial properties or scent). Choose products that are not tested on animals, with ingredients using renewable resources (wherever possible) and with minimal packaging. Avoid anything that contains the following ingredients:

✄ **LANOLIN**: this is extracted from the processed wool of both dead and live animals.

✄ **TITANIUM DIOXIDE**: a colouring agent, this enhances soaps and makes them look clearer.

✄ **CHEMICAL PLASTICISERS**: these are added to soaps to make them easier to mould.

✄ **SYNTHETIC PERFUMES**: these are cheap substitutes for natural oils, perfumes and essences.

✄ **FORMALDEHYDE**: traditionally used to preserve corpses, this will prolong the life of some products.

✄ **SYNTHETIC DYES**: these are used to make a product look more appealing.

✄ **SODIUM TALLOWATE**: this is made from water, caustic soda and the fat from dead animals.

✄ **GLYCERINE**: unless the label says otherwise, this is derived from the carcasses of dead animals.

BUYING
ORGANIC

QUESTIONS
& ANSWERS

Q What is the advantage of choosing organic clothing?

A *Organic fabrics are produced in ways that do not harm the environment or exploit the people who make them. Some 40 per cent of all conventionally grown cotton in the US is genetically engineered. In addition, the conventional cultivation of fibres (such as cotton) consumes huge numbers of agrochemicals. The raw materials of organic clothing are grown organically, and the clothes do not receive chemical textile finishes or treatments. All dyes are either plant- or mineral-derived or are low-impact dyes; all materials are Fair Trade (see page 37).*

Q Are organic supermarkets certified?

A *At present shops are not officially certified by recognised bodies, although this may change in the future. When choosing a retail outlet, look at their policies and ethics, and make sure that they can provide certification for any products they sell that claim to be organic. Many organic supermarkets stock mainly pre-packaged goods with official organic kite-marks.*

Q How can paint be organic?

A *There are a number of organic and eco-friendly paints on the market. They differ from conventional products as follows: all polluting chemicals and toxic emissions are kept to an absolute minimum; colourants are entirely natural and subjected to minimum processing; fillers are powdered marble, dolomite and chalk, all common geological materials; solvents are normally water and vinegar, or citrus-based oils; organic paints contain no petroleum solvents, vinyl or chlorinated polymers; they have a lower odour and help to reduce atmospheric pollution.*

Q Are box schemes cheaper than supermarkets?

A *They often are. In fact, a* Sunday Times *article in the UK pointed out the following: 'The organic price premium is being destabilised by independent organic co-operatives, which sell produce direct – often from the same farmers who supply the supermarkets – at prices up to 44 per cent lower.'*

Q Why should nutritional supplements be organic?

A Because many nutritional supplements are derived from farmed products, they have been subject to intensive farming methods, including pesticide treatments and herbicides. Non-organic supplements may also contain GM ingredients and sugar substitutes (such as aspartame). And some supplements, such as fish oils, are derived from farmed animals. Because toxins are stored in the fat of these animals, you will be getting a whacking dose of chemicals in your supplement, so you are much better off choosing organic supplements.

Q How ethical is it to import organic goods?

A Transporting food from around the world is a cause of pollution and great energy expenditure. It also has the potential to take business away from local farmers. But there are mitigating circumstances: anything that promotes organic agriculture around the world is important, and you will be doing your bit to increase demand and encourage organic practices in other countries. And there are many imported products that cannot be purchased locally. The best advice is to buy local wherever possible, choosing imported organic goods as a second choice.

Q Most of the goods at my local farmers' market are not organic, but claim to use responsible farming methods. Is this acceptable?

A Remember that it takes at least two years (three in the US) for a farm to be certified organic. Many farmers are in the middle of that conversion process and are, indeed, using organic methods. Ask for evidence of this. Also, many farmers have not bothered to apply for organic status, perhaps because the whole farm is not organic. If they can provide proof that their products basically conform to organic growing principles (see pages 16–19), then these are a good alternative.

Q Are there any products that cannot be organic?

A Theoretically, no. Guidelines are currently being drawn up to cover every possible product that consumers require, although these will obviously differ, depending on the purpose or the products. All foods (both vegetable and animal) can be farmed organically, and products used for personal and home hygiene can be produced to meet organic specifications. The focus is on chemical-free, natural, environmentally friendly, fairly traded products, and every manufacturer has the responsibility – and ability – to provide that.

Q Are pre-prepared vegetables as good for you as whole vegetables?

A Ready-prepared salads and chopped vegetables are obviously inferior to their fresh, uncut counterparts, but if you don't have time for much food preparation and are unlikely to eat anything fresh unless it is prepared for you, then they make a good alternative. Watch out, however, for any signs of age, such as browning edges on lettuce, dried-out vegetables and excess moisture in the package.

Q Why is organic food more expensive?

A We talk about this issue in more detail later in the book (see pages 122 and 124), but suffice to say that producing good-quality food, usually tended by hand, is a more expensive process. Furthermore, because chemicals are not used to speed up the process and to produce vast quantities of food at lower prices, you will end up with a higher bill. But consider the fact that it's worth paying for something as valuable as good food, and as demand increases, the price is bound to come down.

5 GROWING ORGANIC

You don't have to be a farmer to grow organic. More and more ordinary gardeners are converting to organic practices, for the purposes of benefiting their own health and that of the environment at the same time. Organic gardening does not require vast knowledge of complicated procedures or endless different tools; it simply means gardening naturally, and it involves a basic understanding of the world that exists within your garden.

Turning a portion of your garden over to organic food can be both a delightful pastime and a source of good, nutritious fare. You'll also enjoy the benefits of a mini eco-system that develops in your own back yard.

But organic gardening is much more than a way of growing plants without chemical sprays and artificial fertilisers. It recognises that there are complex systems within the natural world that need to be respected and complied with. That does not mean producing less, or that your produce will be inferior to plants that are grown in a conventional garden. Quite the opposite: by using natural methods you will produce healthy, flourishing plants, a vibrant garden ecosystem, an enticing habitat for wildlife, and food that is safe, delicious and free of chemicals.

Whatever you are planting – from ornamental shrubs and roses to vegetables and herbs in boxes – there are a few simple principles involved. The first is to ensure that you reduce the demands placed on your garden (and, in particular, the soil) by regularly replacing organic matter. You also need to protect seeds while they germinate, using natural methods, and make sure that they have plenty of water and sunlight. The final step is ensuring that pests and diseases are controlled in a way that encourages health and balance in your garden's ecosystem.

One of the mainstays of organic gardening is the compost heap. This creates organic matter that can be reintroduced into the soil to keep it nourished, and to encourage the growth of natural, healthy bacteria and other micro-organisms that play an important role in the health of your soil and, through that, of your plants. Be prepared to use a little manual labour in your organic garden. You cannot rely on sprays and chemicals to do the work for you, so you will need to be vigilant about digging, seeding, pruning, weeding, watering, recycling, composting and covering. The results will be well worth the effort , and your garden will flourish year after year.

WHY GROW ORGANIC?

The organic approach to gardening and farming recognises that the whole environment in which plants grow is much more than the sum of its individual parts, and that all living things are interrelated and interdependent. There are many obvious reasons for growing organic, including encouraging biodiversity and the health of the environment. Other reasons include:

- Producing tasty, fresh food that is free of contamination.
- Recycling household wastes for compost and reuse, and minimising the use of resources.
- Reducing the amount of pesticides and fertilisers that are polluting our water.
- Encouraging a multitude of wild flowers and wildlife to grow at a local level.
- Saving from extinction old varieties of fruit, flowers and vegetables, many of which are no longer commercially grown.
- Guarding and even increasing the living organisms in the soil, which in turn produces healthier plants that are more resistant to disease and to pests.
- Supporting wildlife in your garden and the surrounding environment, including birds, frogs, toads and smaller creatures, such as worms and ladybirds.
- Creating a safe and pleasant environment in which to work and play. This is particularly important if you have children. Chemical sprays and other products can harm small children, who are more susceptible to poisons than adults are. They are also more likely to touch and eat things in the process of learning and playing. Children can play safely in an organic garden, and can become involved in the pleasures of helping a living space to flourish.
- Getting plenty of pleasure, exercise and fresh air as you work in your garden.

Organic gardening is simple, and you can be confident that the produce you grow is free of chemicals. Get to know your garden: the soil, the natural predators and the helpful plants.

ORGANIC GARDENING BASICS

No matter how big your garden or window box, you can garden organically to create a natural environment in which plants can thrive. Remember that plants grow anyway – all you need to do is give them a helping hand.

SOIL

The most important factor in any organic garden is the fertility of your soil. Get it right and you will produce healthy, delicious crops and thriving flowers and shrubs. Conventional gardeners use a wide range of chemicals to fertilise their plants, but organic gardeners do things differently. The soil is fed rather than supplemented, with organic matter, which includes manure, compost and other organic materials. These encourage worms (see page 78) and the micro-organisms required to keep the soil balanced and fertile.

Not everyone can produce enough compost for their gardens and you may need to use some fertilisers, but these should conform to organic standards. Your local garden shop should have a good selection of products (one of the best is blood, fish and bonemeal). The rate at which you apply these depends on what you want to plant, so get a good organic gardening book for the appropriate recommendations. Some plants will require special treatment: tomatoes may need a potash fertiliser, while leafy vegetables may need extra nitrogen towards the end of the winter months.

COMPOST

Compost is a magnificently versatile and nutritious material, and if you can produce enough, you are unlikely to need another fertiliser. It is exactly what nature manufactures to feed plant life and looks like rich, dark soil. It is made of recycled kitchen and garden waste and is used to feed and condition the earth, and in making potting mixes. Any organic matter – that is, material that was once living – will break down, transferring its nutrients to the compost. These nutrients are then recycled to nourish other plants. Remember, however, that you need a variety of materials to provide a balance of nutrients (see box).

Although it is not essential for your compost heap to be 'hot' in order to decompose and produce good-quality compost, heat does speed up the process. For 'hot' composts, add some activators (see box); don't be alarmed by the use of animal and bird manure or blood – the heat kills off any disease that may be carried in them.

As the materials become available, put them into a covered compost bin or make a pile in the open air. Whichever method you use, it is essential that the bottom of the bin or heap is open and in contact with the earth, so that micro-organisms from the soil are attracted to it. Water the heap from time to time to provide sufficient moisture for correct composting. If you are using an open-air heap, turn it over regularly to hasten the decomposition process. The heap may become hot as the material starts to decompose – this is a sign that it is curing well. As it cools, worms will arrive to finish off the work (see page 78). Compost can be made in six to eight weeks, or it may take a year or more. In general, the more effort you put into making it, the quicker you will get your compost. When the heap is completely cold and the material is fully broken down, it can be applied to your soil.

COMPOSTING MATERIAL

Materials that add heat (to activate the compost) include:

- comfrey leaves
- yarrow
- young weeds
- grass cuttings
- chicken manure
- pigeon manure

Excellent composting materials include:

- fruit and vegetable scraps
- teabags
- coffee grounds
- old flowers
- bedding plants
- old straw and hay
- vegetable plant remains
- strawy manures
- young hedge clippings
- autumn leaves
- cardboard
- cardboard tubes
- gerbil, hamster and rabbit bedding

Other compostable items include:

- paper towels and bags
- perennial weeds
- sawdust
- soft prunings

Slow rotters include:

- tough hedge clippings
- wood ash
- wood shavings
- woody prunings

Avoid composting:

- meat
- fish
- newspaper
- cooked food

Never compost:

- cat litter
- coal and coke ash
- disposable nappies
- dog faeces
- glossy magazines

MULCHING

This effective technique is used by organic and conventional growers alike. You can mulch all year, but it is particularly important in the spring, when seedlings are developing, and in the autumn, to keep the ground warm enough to sustain growth during winter. Mulch is any organic matter that covers the soil. In the forest, for instance, the soil is covered with leaves, twigs and bark, which lie undisturbed and then decay, nourishing the earth. Mulching also excludes light to prevent weeds from appearing. Organic gardeners endeavour to reproduce these conditions using a variety of organic matter:

◆ HAY: this is one of the best mulches to use, as the deep roots of grass take up minerals and other nutrients, which are often unavailable to shallow-rooted plants. They are then transferred to your soil as the hay decomposes. You can actually now purchase spoiled hay that has already started to decompose.

◆ LEAVES: these make a very good mulch, as they are similar to the natural forest mulch.

◆ BARK: this can be chipped or shredded, and is available in a variety of different grades of coarseness, but can be expensive.

◆ GRASS CUTTINGS: these are effective as a mulch for weed control, but must be freshly mown and at least 15cm/6in deep. If they are layered too thickly, the air will not reach the soil. Grass can also become slimy, which makes it useless as a soil conditioner.

◆ PEAT AND COMPOST: about 5–7cm /2–3in of a loose material like peat provides a good soil conditioner and an inhospitable home for weed seedlings. Compost is fine, but a very thick layer is required to prevent weeds.

HOW AND WHY TO MULCH

Ensure that your soil is well watered and that whatever nutrients you intend to add to the soil (such as compost or bonemeal) have been applied. Place your mulch over the soil in fairly thick layers, so that all of the bare earth is fully covered. Plant seedlings by moving aside the mulch, leaving a couple of centimetres/an inch or so free around each plant. The main benefits gained from mulching are:

- weed control
- water conservation
- root-temperature control
- encouragement of worms (see page 78)
- addition of nutrients to the soil

CROP ROTATION

This is the practice of alternating plants that are grown in a planned sequence in successive crop years. Organic certification programmes require 'soil-building' crop rotations, meaning that they must be specifically designed to steadily improve soil fertility, while reducing nitrate-leaching into the ground, weed, pest and disease problems.

A good rotation plan allows efficient use of your garden and minimises disease. By using legumes (pulses such as beans and peas) appropriately you will also keep up the soil's fertility. The basic principle involves moving vegetables around between plots, incorporating some legumes and growing some 'green manure' crops (see box). The best rotation system is achieved by dividing your garden into four roughly equal areas and planting them with four groups of vegetables, then moving them at the end of each year.

Try to group crops so that brassicas are together. Tomatoes and potatoes should be in the same bed or, if in separate beds, do not let them follow each other in the rotation plan. Carrots, celery, parsley and parsnips should be kept together, as should onions, garlic, shallots and leeks. The legumes should be grown in the same bed. The idea is to leave two or three years before returning a crop to a plot where you first grew it.

> ### GREEN MANURE
>
> Green manure is an effective own-grown compost material and includes any plant grown as temporary ground cover, with the aim of improving fertility. It is normally grown on vacant soil over the winter, or in between crops. It helps to prevent soil erosion and the leaching of nutrients, and to convert otherwise wasted winter sunlight into compost. It is then dug into the ground to enhance the soil's organic content. Good examples of green manure plants include beans and peas, lupins, clover, trefoil, fenugreek, buckwheat, mustard and fodder radish (produced for animal feed).

Low netting tunnels and cages will help to protect plants from birds, rabbits and other animal pests. Make sure, however, that the netting is not too fine. Bees and other insects will need access to do their work!

PEST CONTROL

There are several methods of pest control that are approved by organic organisations, and most of them are easy to put in place. Companion planting is discussed in detail on pages 74–75. Rotation planting is another method (see page 71): if you move plants each season, then pests and diseases in the soil re-emerge in the spring to find a particular species gone.

ENCOURAGING NATURAL
PREDATORS AND PARASITES

Ensure that you have a healthy ecosystem in your garden with a wide variety of different plants: plants for nectar, fruit and pollen; plants offering shelter, sites for nests and water; and, vitally important, some plants that you are prepared to sacrifice! On these you can maintain colonies of pests on which predators and parasites can feed.

Companion planting deters pests or disease, and encourages healthy predators. Plants grow better when they are with like-minded flora!

BARRIERS AND TRAPS

There are many ways in which you can exclude pests until they reach the point where they are few enough not to cause problems. Nets can protect plants on the ground – even a stocking will do, or you can buy fine netting, woven horticultural fleeces or punctured plastic sheets to keep pests off vegetables and fruit; they can also prevent problems such as carrot-root fly.

Birds can be distracted by using scarecrows, glitter bangs (pieces of tin foil tied along string) or even rows of black cotton, set up in a spider's web across your plants. Birds are clever, though, and you will have to change the placing and type of your scarer on a regular basis, or they will get wise to it.

Traps are even more versatile. Use a carpet to seal larger areas of soil, trapping insects underneath when they emerge. If you lay it on wet soil, you will bring up soil pests overnight and they can be swept away or left for the birds in the morning. Sticky boards and flypapers are useful in the greenhouse, particularly for catching whitefly and thrips. When they are hung in fruit trees, they can also reduce the moth population.

Tins buried in the ground with bits of food, such as potato, attract millipedes and woodlice, while slugs and snails are drawn to rotting fruit and wireworms to bran. Make the tins deep enough that the pests will become trapped, ready for later collection. And there are humane mouse-traps that allow you to release the animals later. Place them near peas, beans or crocuses, which mice love.

HAND-PICKING

Time-consuming as this may seem, picking off pests by hand is an effective way of controlling them. You can use this method for sawfly, caterpillars, slugs and snails. Or use an outdoor vacuum cleaner (such as one designed to collect leaves) and literally suck pests off foliage. A water hose with a strong jet can knock aphids and other pests from many plants.

BUYING IN PREDATORS AND PARASITES

It sounds extraordinary, but you can buy predators by mail order in most parts of the Western world. This technique is most suitable for greenhouses, where the predators won't fly away. *Aphidoletes aphidimyza* is a parasitic midge used to control aphids. *Cryptolaemus montrouzieri* is a ladybird whose larvae control mealy bugs. Caterpillars can be killed with naturally occurring bacterial diseases, such as *Bacillus thuringiensis*, which is sprayed on plants. Look at a good gardening catalogue for details.

ORGANIC PESTICIDES

There are natural pesticides that conform to organic standards. They are, however, a last resort, and great care must be taken to avoid disrupting the ecosystem of your garden. Bees are particularly in danger when pesticides are used, and are essential for pollination.

One of the best natural pesticides is soft soap, which can be used to kill aphids, spider mite, whitefly and other pests. Other pesticides include quassia solution (made from tree bark), pyrethrum (only available at present in the US, and made from the flower heads of chrysanthemums) and derris (extracted from tropical plants). You can use Bordeaux mixture for potato blight, raspberry-cane spot and other fungal diseases; and sulphur to control powdery mildews and to prevent rot in winter bulbs and tubers.

Ladybirds and their grey larvae eat large quantities of aphids. While they cannot be attracted to a garden by specific plants, they can be encouraged by planting a wide selection of flowers and plants.

73

COMPANION PLANTING

This technique involves selecting plants that are known to work well together (see table below), in order to encourage beneficial insects by providing shelter; to discourage pests by the use of aromas; and to create a healthy ecosystem for all of the plants in the garden. Many gardeners believe that some companion plants, such as nettles and alliums (plants of the onion family), when grown in association with a crop, can help to prevent fungal and bacterial attack. For this reason chives and garlic are often grown under fruit and roses. Other plants attract pests away from the main planting: sweet tobacco has sticky stems and leaves and is attractive to whitefly and other insects.

CONTROLLING DISEASE

Creating a healthy organic garden involves a certain amount of vigilance. If you spot signs of mildew, cut off the offending leaf or stem and remove it from the garden. And ensure that the plants you

Plant	Good companions	Bad companions
asparagus	tomato, basil, parsley	potatoes
aubergines	beans, potatoes, marjoram	–
beans	carrots, cabbage, cucumber, cauliflower	leeks, chives, garlic, onions
broad beans	potatoes, lettuce	fennel
bush beans	strawberries, grapes	garlic, onions
dwarf beans	beetroot, kohlrabi	–
beetroot	kohlrabi, dwarf beans, onions, chives	runner/climbing beans, lettuce, silverbeet, cabbage, leaf mustard
broccoli	dill, celery, chamomile, sage, rosemary	tomatoes, strawberries, oregano
Brussels sprouts	potatoes, sage, hyssop, thyme	strawberries, rosemary
cabbage	beetroot, potatoes, beans, onions, sage	tomatoes, garlic, strawberries, celery, dill, mint, thyme, oregano
capsicum	basil	–

Plant	Good companions	Bad companions
carrots	leeks, lettuce, onions, peas, tomatoes	dill, parsnip, chives, sage, rosemary, radish
cauliflower	celery, celeriac, beans, oregano	strawberries, rue, peas, potatoes, nasturtium
celery	leeks, beans, cabbage, tomatoes	parsnip, potatoes, wheat
corn	melons, squash, pumpkins, cucumbers, potatoes, parsnips, artichokes, Jerusalem artichokes	–
courgettes	corn, marjoram, nasturtium	–
cucumber	beans, peas, radish, celery, carrots	potatoes, sage, cauliflower, basil
chives	carrots, tomatoes, parsley, parsnips, fruit trees	–
horseradish	potatoes, fruit trees	–
kohlrabi	beetroot, onions, dwarf beans	pole beans, tomatoes, cucumber
leeks	carrots, celery, celeriac, strawberries	–

buy (or grow from seed) are healthy. Although that may sound obvious, it may be necessary to ask for a certification number to show that a plant is free from disease. Keep your greenhouse scrupulously clean and be ruthless about weeding, digging and pest control. When plants become weakened, they are more susceptible to pests and disease. The aim is to ensure your plants are healthy enough to withstand anything. The table on the right shows some of the most common plant diseases and their organic treatments.

Plant	Good companions	Bad companions
lettuce	strawberries, cabbage, carrots, onions	parsley, beans, beetroot, parsnip
nasturtium	cabbage, cauliflower, cucumber	broccoli, Brussels sprouts potatoes, radish, squash, courgettes, fruit trees
onions	cabbage, carrots, beetroot, lettuce	beans, peas, parsnip, parsley, leeks
peas	carrots, corn, cucumber, beans, radish	onions, garlic, shallots
potatoes	beans, corn, cabbage, horseradish	pumpkin, squash, cucumber, dill, eggplant, tomatoes, raspberries
pumpkin	corn, marjoram	potatoes
radish	cucumber, lettuce, kohlrabi, melon	hyssop, squash, peas, nasturtium
spinach	broad beans, strawberries, fruit trees	–
tomatoes	asparagus, basil, lima beans, cabbage	beetroot, fennel, broccoli, kohlrabi, Brussels sprouts, cauliflower, potatoes, rosemary, carrots, chives, dill, onions, parsley, etc.

DISEASE TREATMENTS

Problem	Treatments
Grey mould (botrytis) appears as brown spotting or blotching, followed by furry, grey mould.	Avoid overwatering, wet mulches and planting in shady areas; cut off infected shoots and burn them.
Powdery mildews look like a mealy, pale-grey coating on leaves, buds, flowers and shoots, causing yellowing.	Ensure that your plants and the soil don't become overdamp; spray with copper fungicide, and hand-water plants; cut off and burn any leaves showing disease.
Sooty mould is a black fungus that grows on the sticky secretions of pests such as aphids.	Controlling the pests will solve the problem.
Rust appears in many different forms, and may be yellow, red, brown or black.	Remove and burn any leaves with spots; spray the plant with dispersible sulphur; in a greenhouse, keep the humidity levels down.
Wilts and rots are caused by organisms that live in the soil and they tend to attack unhealthy plants.	Ensure that you use a good compost, rich in micro-organisms that will attack the offending organisms.

Good, crumbly, rich soil is a must for successful organic gardening in a window box, or in beds. Not only is it a home for millions of living organisms, which provide the right conditions for plant growth, but it provides your plants with food in the form they can best ingest.

GROWING FRUIT AND VEGETABLES, FLOWERS AND SHRUBS

There are literally hundreds of different fruit and vegetables that can safely and easily be grown in an organic garden, but in most gardens space is at a premium. The best way to choose what to plant is to select fruit and vegetables that your family will use and enjoy.

All of the methods of organic gardening will need to be undertaken – that means preparing the soil carefully, using a rotation programme, and buying good-quality seeds that are certified by a reputable organic organisation. Remember that fruit-growing takes up a lot of space, so check the label carefully to ensure that you give every plant sufficient room to flourish. Also check that your chosen varieties are self-fertile or capable of pollinating each other, or you may find that you have a disappointing crop. Buy a soil-testing kit to work out whether the plants you intend to grow will survive, and ensure that your plants are appropriate for the weather conditions in your garden. Talk to a good specialist grower for advice.

Most organic gardeners recommend intercropping vegetables to make the most of a plot. This means growing fast-growing, fast-maturing plants in between rows of slow-growing, slow-maturing plants. The first crop will be harvested long before the slower-growing plants require the space. This also gives you a fairly continuous supply of vegetables.

Fruit trees need to be pruned regularly, not only to ensure a good yield, but also to help keep the trees free of pests and diseases. Prune out the old wood and cut down to a healthy, outward-facing bud, angling the cut so that the rain will not penetrate and encourage disease. Prune in both the winter and the summer: winter pruning stimulates replacement growth, while summer pruning stimulates fruiting. Protect soft fruit (such as currants and berries) and bush and cane fruit with nets to keep the birds away.

Choose vegetables based on your needs. In a small garden you might want to choose carrots, salads and climbing peas and beans. If you don't have much time on your hands, choose courgettes, squash, beans and potatoes, which all require relatively little work and attention. Onions and garlic are equally easy to grow, provided that you are careful about keeping weeds away. Vegetable crops should be rotated regularly (see page 71). Always choose plants that are compatible with one another.

FLOWERS AND SHRUBS

Flowers are an important part of any organic garden, not only because they add colour and beauty, but because they provide nectar and pollen for beneficial insects, such as bees. Use a wide variety of flowers to ensure a good range of beneficial insects and other creatures. You need to aim for a rich selection of different-coloured and different-perfumed flowers, plenty of fresh green foliage and berries; some permanent plants, such as trees; shrubs and perennials; bulbs that flower in different seasons; annual and biennial bedding plants for extra colour; and even some vegetables. You also need a good blend of winter and summer plants.

Always begin by planting the shrubs. Herbaceous plants can be slotted in later, and moved if necessary. Roses are a good choice of shrub, adding colour as well as encouraging beneficial pests. Bulbs, annuals and biennials will tolerate most soil conditions and light levels. Most organic gardening experts recommend raising flower beds above the level of your lawn to improve drainage. Add plenty of organic matter (compost) and grit to the soil when digging.

Consider some hedging, to provide shelter from the wind, although in a small garden a fence or wall will do. Climbing plants growing along a wall or fence help to break the wind and filter the air, keeping the climate within the garden more temperate. Shrubs provide a home for birds, butterflies and other insects, so it is a good idea to choose some with berries. Always aim for a few native plants, to encourage natural wildlife.

If you have a small garden, you can grow different herbs and vegetables side by side. You can plant the herbs in rows or use them as an ornamental border.

LAWNS, CONTAINERS AND HERBS

It is definitely possible to have an organic lawn. Most families with children require a lawn of some sort, and you will feel a lot more confident about allowing your children to play in an organic garden, which is free of nasty chemicals.

The most important element of organic lawn gardening is preparing the site. You need healthy, fertile soil, with plenty of worms (see box) and other micro-organisms. Worms are particularly important because they aerate the soil, and their casts help to break down the nutrients into a form that is more readily available to plants. Use organic manure and compost as you dig the site, then add a good layer of gravel under heavy soil to improve the drainage. To keep the soil aerated and to improve drainage or water retention (as necessary), work over the lawn with a hollow-tined fork, removing small cores of soil. You can then fill these with organic grit and compost. Brush any earthworm casts around the lawn with a stiff broom.

Cut your lawn in opposite directions, on alternate cuts. Don't be tempted to cut it too closely, or you will encourage bare patches, which may then be colonised by moss and weeds. Remove the cuttings to prevent a build-up of dead material, which is susceptible to fungi. Rake the lawn with a heavy rake at least once a year in order to remove all dead grass.

SEED OR TURF?

You can either sow your garden from seed or, for a more 'instant' lawn, you can now purchase organic turf, which obviously gives a much faster result. Always buy it from a reliable source to ensure a good-quality finish.

Lawns can be fed in two ways: you can use slow-release blood, fish and bonemeal once or twice in early spring, and then again in summer, or you can apply a liquid-manure feed that is high in nitrogen. Liquid seaweed is a good choice for organic gardens. Keep weeds under control by cutting them out with a knife, or by dropping table salt at their base.

WORMS

Worms are crucial to the success of a healthy garden. They live on organic matter and process it by eating it and providing worm casts that nourish the soil. As they tunnel they aerate and break up the soil. If you give them plenty of organic matter on which to feast, your soil will become more productive.

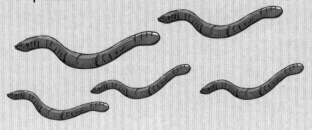

CONTAINER GARDENING

The key to any successful container is the soil; it tires easily and will need plenty of feeding on a regular basis with compost or organic liquid fertiliser. The second key is drainage. If there are no holes in the base of your pots, drill them yourself. Before replanting any container, remove the top 23cm/9in and mix in some well-rotted garden compost or manure. Then refill and plant. Avoid putting anything too tall in a container garden, unless you have a trellis or some other means of support.

Prepare containers well before planting them up for the first time. Place some broken pots, concave side down, over the drainage holes. Cover them with gravel, then a piece of turf or some old sacking. This will prevent the compost from clogging up the drainage holes. Put in a layer of manure or compost, then top up the container with soil. Always allow at least 3.5cm/1½in of space at the top for watering.

HERBS

Some herbs need to be planted on their own, while others thrive when planted together. Plant rosemary, bay and mint on their own. Chives, sage, coriander, parsley, marjoram and thyme work well with other herbs. Give shrubby types a pot of their own, or make sure that you prune them regularly. All herbs need ample sun and a well-drained soil, so container gardening is normally your best bet.

If you do plant herbs in the ground, make sure that the site is very well drained. Add organic matter and large quantities of grit, and raise the beds slightly to encourage drainage. Double-dig the area, breaking up the subsoil and working in the organic matter. Spread a mulch of well-rotted compost or manure over the top of the whole garden to encourage and maintain fertility, and to discourage slugs. Make sure that the herbs are given plenty of water – preferably using a sprinkler, which ensures that the water permeates through to the lower levels. Hand-weeding is essential, while hand-picking will control most pests.

Use plants, tubs or window boxes to grow herbs, or to fill a barren part of your garden. Never use a peat-based compost in a container, as it dries out quickly and you have to be extremely vigilant with the watering can.

GROWING
ORGANIC
10
QUESTIONS
&ANSWERS

Q Do I need to buy a special composter for my garden?

A No, any container will do, as long as it is open at the base and in contact with the earth. Some gardeners don't even bother with a container, simply adding compost material to a heap and ensuring that it is turned over regularly. You can cover your pile with recyclable garden refuse bags to encourage the production of heat. All compost heaps need water and regular turning.

Q Can I add diseased plants to my compost container?

A The decaying process should destroy any disease in the compost, so theoretically it is fine to add them to your compost. However, persistent diseases, such as white rot and club root, are best avoided. Grey mould, mildews and wilt may survive in a slow, cool heap, but the microbial activity should dispose of almost everything.

Q Do you have any tips for growing organic potatoes?

A Always buy seed potatoes that are certified virus-free. It can be tempting to use potatoes that are sprouting in your larder, but these may contain viruses. Avoid growing potatoes on very alkaline soils or on soil that you have limed. Lime encourages scab disease, and if scab is a problem, choose varieties (such as Maris Peer) that are resistant. If your crop suffers from blight you can use a copper-based spray as a last resort, but you are better off trying to grow resistant varieties. If blight does strike, destroy the damaged stems to stop the spores spreading.

Q How can I prevent carrot fly?

A Cover the area with horticultural fleece, to stop the flies laying eggs close to the crop. Alternatively, a high fine-mesh fence should prevent the fly from damaging the carrots. Recently manured soil can increase the chance of root deformities in carrots, so well-prepared, deeply dug soil is essential. Delay sowing the carrots until early summer, and harvest them before late summer. Always rotate your crops. It is also helpful to grow onions, leeks, garlic or shallots next to them, or in the same bed, which seems to deter carrot flies.

Q I can't seem to grow roses successfully using organic methods. Do you have any tips?

A Check all plants for signs of mildew and black spot before buying them. Roses need to be heavily pruned (every year in early spring) by cutting all the shoots back to an outward- or downward-facing bud. If you have a rose sucker, scrape away a little soil where the sucker arises from the root and pull it off; if you cannot do this, cut it as near to the stem as possible. Always deadhead roses. Feed them regularly with good-quality compost and manure, and mulch them. They need to be watered well in warm weather.

Q No matter how much compost I put on, my soil doesn't seem to be nutritious enough to grow anything that looks very healthy. What is happening?

A Soil preparation is essential. Get rid of all the perennial weeds. If you have a real problem, grow a 'cleaning' crop such as potatoes and wait a year before converting the ground. Double-dig the entire garden to aerate the top soil and break up the subsoil. Incorporate some manure and compost at a rate of 10–15kg/22–33lb per sq m/yd. If your soil is heavy and badly drained, raise the borders. Look out for signs of disease on existing plants and treat them accordingly.

Q Are there any 'good' weeds?

A It is important to remember that weeds are plants, too – they are just growing in the wrong place! Any piece of ground will rapidly be covered with weeds if left untended, and these compete with each other until some species begin to dominate. In the long-term weeds do build up the fertility of the soil as they decompose. Some deep-rooted weeds, such as dock and thistle, bring up nutrients from deep within the earth, making them available for future crops. Chickweed, dock, forget-me-nots, goose-grass and yarrow can all add to the ecosystem in your garden.

Q Will my compost heap attract rats?

A One of the reasons why no cooked foods or meat should be added to a compost heap is because they attract rats. If you do have rats in your area, they will undoubtedly be attracted to compost. In this case it is probably best to use a sealed compost container. A predatory cat will help to solve the problem!

Q There is a big wasp nest in my garden. How can I get rid of it organically?

A Wasps are actually useful early in the season, because they hunt other insects. However, they will need to be trapped later on, when fruit starts appearing. You can fill a bottle half full of water and jam, capping it with foil containing just a small hole. The wasps can crawl in, but cannot fly out again. Avoid using these near flowers, as you may catch bees instead. If you can find the nest, flood it or puff derris dust into the entrance.

Q How can I get rid of the weeds in my lawn?

A Regular mowing kills almost all of the tall-growing weeds. Acid-loving weeds can be discouraged by liming the area with a calcified seaweed or dolomitic lime twice a year. Use a wire rake in the autumn or spring to scarify, or break up, the grass. Regularly rake in a mixture of ground seaweed, rock dust and grass seed with sharp sand (for heavy soils) and lime or calcified seaweed (for acid soils) in the spring to encourage healthy grass that will win out over common weeds and health problems.

6 COOKING ORGANIC

One of the delights of organic food is its taste. Throughout this book we have focused on the health and environmental benefits of eating organic food, without paying due attention to the fact that it tastes infinitely better. And because it is tastier, organic food does not need to be cooked to death and smothered with seasonings and sauces. In fact, lightly steamed or even raw organic vegetables can form the basis of your diet, putting much less strain on your body and ensuring that you have all the vitamins and minerals you need for optimum health.

Many people find that, after switching to organic produce, conventionally grown produce tends to taste bland and the texture is often unappealing. For this reason many of us (children especially) find it hard to meet the recommended intake of five to seven servings of fruit and vegetables each day.

Organic produce is different. For example, organic tomatoes tend to be sweeter and less woody than their conventionally grown counterparts; non-organic broccoli tends to be bland and rubbery, whereas the organic alternative is crisp and flavour-rich; organic carrots are firm and naturally sweet; organic apples are crisp and juicy. You are much more likely to include delicious vegetables and fruit in your daily diet if they are a pleasure to eat. And when you find that fresh produce is so appealing, you are more likely to try different varieties and to experiment with what is on offer.

Use whole organic foods in cooking whenever possible for maximum nutritional value. The less you cook them, the tastier and more nutritious they will be.

Many consumers have opted for a diet that is heavily processed and pre-packaged, partly because of convenience, but partly because preparing a palatable meal from an unappealing selection of foods is often too difficult to contemplate. This is where organic food comes into its own. For those who have opted for organic produce because of its health benefits, the improved taste comes as a pleasant surprise. However, it is important to remember that healthy food is only nutritious if it is prepared and cooked properly. On pages 57 and 59 we looked at how to choose fresh produce. In this section we focus on how to prepare organic food to get the very most from it.

YOUR ORGANIC KITCHEN

Cooking organic food requires relatively little work, but there are a few useful kitchen tools that will ensure that the everyday food you prepare is full of natural vitamins and minerals and that its natural taste is preserved:

A steamer is an excellent accessory, allowing you to cook fruit and vegetables quickly and to preserve their nutrients. You can also use it to cook rice, meat and other foods without the need for unhealthy fats.

A juicer can be used to prepare delicious fruit and vegetable juices. This is an excellent way to get the most from your fresh produce, as the nutrients are concentrated. If you have picky eaters in your family, it is also a great way to ensure that everyone gets the nutrients they need from fresh fruit and vegetables. Try orange and cucumber, apple and celery, kiwi and pear or mango and carrot juices. Always dilute freshly squeezed juice (by at least half and half) with water to ensure that your blood-sugar levels remain stable – fresh fruit and vegetables are naturally sweet!

A blender is handy for puréeing lightly cooked fruit and vegetables into nutritious soups and sauces.

A chopping board is essential, but choose one made from FSC (Forestry Stewardship Council) sustainable wood; use a separate chopping board for meat.

Plenty of trays for freezing are needed. If you grow your own organic produce it should really be frozen on the day that it is picked. Herbs can be chopped and frozen in ice-cube trays with a squirt of water, to provide a cheap and readily available supply of tasty nutrients and flavours.

A wok is an extremely useful tool. Lightly stir-frying organic food helps to preserve its nutrients and makes a quick and efficient way of cooking.

FRESH OR FROZEN?

The old adage that 'fresh is best' no longer holds true in our world of supermarkets and one-stop convenience shopping. If you are lucky enough to purchase produce that was picked on the same day, you can be sure that it is full of nutrients. However, the longer food sits in the back of a lorry or on a supermarket shelf, the less likely it is to be nutritious. So what's the answer? Frozen food.

Let me qualify that. Choosing local organic produce not only has environmental implications (see page 54), but is more likely to offer freshness than, say, buying an organic banana from the Caribbean. Second best is frozen, as frozen fruit and vegetables are processed immediately after harvest. Some experts claim that key nutrients are destroyed by freezing, but overall frozen fruit and vegetables are a good choice, particularly if you are too busy to get to the shops on a daily basis.

HOW LONG CAN I KEEP FRESH FOOD?

Luckily we have refrigerators to prevent foods from spoiling too quickly, and keeping food at cool temperatures can help to preserve its nutritional value. However, even organic foods are often picked before they reach peak ripeness, and you will need some warmth (ideally some sunlight) to ensure that they ripen properly. Don't stash a whole load of organic produce in your refrigerator – its taste and health benefits will be compromised. If you can, buy your organic food two or three times a week and eat it as soon as possible. You can tell when food has gone past its best – vegetables become soft or rubbery, fruit soft and oversweet, and milk and meat very obviously go off. When you choose to go organic, you need to become more organised about shopping and rotating food in your larder or refrigerator so that it is eaten while still fresh. However, if you cannot eat fresh produce in time, freeze it on the day you buy it.

Unless you are lucky enough to be able to pick food fresh from your garden or farm, or to get it from a market, it's likely to have been sitting around for some time. Supermarket fare will have lost much of its nutritional value while being packaged and transported.

PREPARING FROZEN PRODUCE

Frozen fruit and vegetables normally require less cooking than fresh because they have often been quickly blanched (immersed in boiling water) before freezing. Use a steamer, or stir them into soups or stews.

Wash vegetables thoroughly in cold water. You can peel or trim vegetables before freezing, but it is not essential. An important step in preparing vegetables for freezing is heating or 'blanching' before packing. Almost all vegetables, except green peppers, maintain better quality if blanched before freezing. If vegetables are not sufficiently blanched, the enzymes continue to be active during frozen storage and the vegetables may develop off-flavours, discolour or toughen.

To blanch, use a pot with a fitted colander, heat the water to boiling and then lower the vegetables into the water with the colander. As soon as the vegetable's colour intensifies, remove from the water and plunge into a basin of ice-cold water. Blanching time varies with the vegetable and size of the pieces: a good rule of thumb is to watch for the colour to heighten. For example, carrots need only 30 seconds before they turn a bright orange, while beans may need a minute or two. A good cookbook will provide you with guidance.

Most fruit can be frozen satisfactorily, but the quality of the frozen product will vary with the kind of fruit, and its ripeness. Wash all fruit in cold water before packing. Wash a small quantity at a time to save undue handling, which may bruise delicate fruit, such as berries. In general, fruit is prepared for freezing in the same way as for serving. Large fruit are generally better if cut into pieces or crushed before freezing. Freeze on baking trays until just solid, and then transfer to individual, sealed bags. A good way to make use of frozen fruit is in a nutritious summer pudding.

Ideally, most fruit and vegetables should be used within a month of freezing; however, they will still be nutritionally sound for up to six months.

STORING FOOD

One of the most important safety points is the temperature of your refrigerator. Too cold, and the food will partly freeze, causing damage. Too warm, and the food may not be properly chilled, allowing bacteria to flourish. The coldest part of the refrigerator should be at 0–5°C/32–41°F.

Bear in mind that refrigerators do not kill bacteria. Food should only be refrigerated for a short time. Milk lasts two or three days, but meat should not be kept for longer than 48 hours, and poultry for just 24. Fresh fish should only be refrigerated for 12 hours before it becomes a health hazard.

Remove fruit and vegetables from their plastic bags to prevent moisture build-up.

Frozen foods are labelled with a star system, which tells you how long they can safely be frozen. One star means a week, two stars a month and three stars three months.

Keep your freezer temperature down to -18°C/0°F. A full freezer helps you to do this, but purchase a freezer thermometer to check the temperature regularly.

When preparing organic food, you need to observe the same standards of hygiene in the kitchen. Use a separate chopping board for meats and vegetables, and keep your work surfaces clean.

PREPARING FOODS

The way you prepare your food is just as important as the food that you choose. Because organic food is so much tastier, you can serve as much of it as possible raw. Even hot meals can be served with a raw fruit and vegetable salad on the side, and nutritious soups and casseroles can have vegetables added at the last minute in order to preserve their nutrients.

TOP TIPS FOR PREPARING ORGANIC FOOD

◆ Scrubbing vegetables is better than peeling, since many valuable vitamins and minerals lie just beneath their skins.

◆ Never soak vegetables for long periods. Wash them briefly under running water, so that you don't let the water-soluble vitamins (such as vitamins B and C) leach out of them.

◆ Grill food whenever possible. It allows you to cook without the use of fat, and helps to maintain the nutritional content of the food.

◆ Cut down on the overall amount of fat that you use in your cooking. Browning meat and vegetables in a non-stick pan is a useful way of drawing out some of the fat in meat, and of changing the flavour of vegetables without actually allowing them to absorb unnecessary fat.

◆ Eat fresh fruit and vegetables raw whenever possible. Just five minutes of boiling reduces the thiamine (a B vitamin) content of peas by up to 40 per cent. Similarly, boiling cabbage reduces its vitamin C content by up to 75 per cent. Although vegetables are a good source of vitamin C, we often end up pouring away most of the nutrients down the sink. Try to cook without water by steaming, stir-frying or microwaving briefly.

◆ Roasting vegetables at a high temperature for a short period of time is a good way to guarantee optimum nutritional content. Ensure they are still slightly crunchy when serving.

◆ Rice should be cooked with the minimum of water, which is absorbed and not discarded. If you have previously been cooking vegetables, use the cooking water for your rice, adding a little lemon juice to reduce the starchiness.

◆ Avoid deep-frying at all cost. Apart from its incredibly high fat content, it destroys almost all the nutrients in food and you will end up with empty calories and a great deal of fat. Heating oils and fats to a high temperature also alters their structure, making them impossible to digest, poisonous and even carcinogenic. This is why it is better not to fry food at high temperatures or to reheat cooking oil. If you must fry food, olive oil is probably the safest, but it should never be heated to smoking point.

◆ Soups and casseroles are an excellent way to preserve nutritional content, as any vitamins and minerals lost in the cooking process are found in the broth.

◆ Lightly grill fish until it is just tender, but no longer raw.

◆ Cook poultry in a slow oven until cooked right through.

◆ Poach fresh seafood gently, in as little water as possible.

◆ Baked potatoes are the most nutritious way to eat this vegetable. Mashed potatoes can be made with the skins on, for optimum nutritional value, but avoid boiling potatoes if possible. If you must have chips, choose fatter ones and oven-bake them. Home-made chips can be delicious. Slice large chunks of potato (with the skin on) and toss in olive oil and a teaspoon of organic sea salt. Bake at a high temperature, turning often, until crisp and brown.

◆ Remember that some of the metal from saucepans and frying pans can leach into food. Copper can cause illness and diarrhoea, and aluminium has been linked with Alzheimer's disease. Stainless-steel or cast-iron pots are fine. Although some of the iron can be absorbed into food, this is not normally problematic. Glass and enamel are safe, and do not react with food.

RAW ENERGY

Here are some easy ideas for serving raw fruit and vegetables:

Juicing (see page 83) provides an easy-to-absorb, concentrated source of nutrients.

A platter of crudités makes a great nutritious snack or the basis of a healthy lunch. Choose a variety of different vegetables and fruit. Make an easy dip using organic crème fraîche blended with chopped organic chives, basil and sundried tomatoes.

Fresh cucumbers, tomatoes, sugarsnap peas and red onions can be tossed in organic olive oil, black pepper, balsamic vinegar and fresh basil to make a delicious salad.

An easy-to-make salsa combines tomatoes, onion, cayenne peppers and coriander. Use it as a side-dish for meats or as a dip for home-made chips or even bread.

WHICH COOKING METHOD?

To limit the damage caused to food by cooking, choose a method that uses as little water and fat as possible. Steaming is your best bet, because nutrients are not leached out during cooking. You can use a colander or a specially designed steaming tray inside a saucepan. Place inside after the water boils, and salt the water slightly. Remove from the heat when the vegetables are crisp and brightly coloured. You can also steam in a double boiler (bain-marie).

Stir-frying at a high temperature also ensures that your food does not lose important nutrients. Choose a good-quality organic olive oil as a base, or use a non-stick pan. Heat the pan to a high temperature before adding the food, and stir constantly. Meat and fish should be cooked first until nearly done, then add vegetables or fruit and cook lightly, until highly coloured and crisp.

Microwaves can be a good method of steaming, but there are several drawbacks. First of all, they are associated with electro-magnetic radiation, which may have health risks. Second, food tends to become cold more quickly, which often means last-minute reheating. Finally, microwaved food continues to cook after it has been removed from the oven, which means that crispy broccoli may be a pulpy mass by the time you serve it.

Roasting vegetables and meat can be a good way of preserving their nutrients, and the juices can be used in gravies or stocks. Roasting vegetables such as potatoes, carrots and peppers whole will ensure that more nutrients are contained in the final product.

Lightly steamed or stir-fried foods, with a little fresh seasoning, are the ideal way to get the most from your organic food.

Remember, fresh vegetables need little cooking. Use sea salt or fresh organic vegetable or fruit juice to bring out the flavour.

GETTING THE MOST
FROM YOUR ORGANIC PRODUCE

There are numerous ways to bring out the flavour of fresh food without adding unhealthy fats or sauces:

◆ Natural sea salt is rich in trace elements and iodine (an essential nutrient). Processed foods contain far too much salt, but if your diet is based on fresh, natural organic foods, you can add some salt without fear of health risks. A starchy dish (such as rice, or potato soup) for four people needs about half a teaspoon of salt. Always add to taste.

◆ Drizzle cold-pressed organic olive oil over vegetables instead of using butter.

◆ Toss vegetables with fresh basil or coriander (or any herb to taste), to enhance their natural flavours.

◆ A little fresh orange juice brings out the flavour of most fruit. Rhubarb loses its sour taste when cooked with orange juice.

◆ Don't hesitate to use freshly squeezed fruit or vegetable juices on lightly cooked fare. Fresh apple juice drizzled over an organic pork roast makes a delightful change to gravy, or purée lightly cooked apples with a little orange juice to make apple sauce. Toss lightly steamed vegetables in carrot, mango or orange juice, or bring out the flavour with a little balsamic vinegar.

◆ Soak fresh sliced garlic and chilli in cold-pressed organic olive oil, then drizzle over meat and lightly cooked vegetables.

◆ Experiment with herbs and spices. Most are now available in organic form, and you need only a little to enhance the flavour.

NUTRIENT LOSSES DURING DIFFERENT METHODS OF COOKING

Method	Nutrients lost
Baking	Some vitamin B (particularly thiamine) and vitamin C.
Boiling	40–70 per cent of vitamin C, plus some vitamin B and potassium.
Canning	30 per cent of vitamins B and C during processing.
Chilling	A little vitamin B and C.
Dehydration	50 per cent of vitamin C and some vitamin A.
Freezing	Most losses are the result of blanching vegetables before freezing; 30 per cent loss of vitamin C; some iron and B vitamins may also be lost from the 'drip' in meat and fish during defrosting.
Grilling and roasting	Some vitamin B and C, but less than in most other cooking methods.
Microwaving	Vitamin C, but less than in conventional cooking; vitamin B losses are similar to those lost in conventional cooking.
Steaming and pressure-cooking	Some vitamin B and C, but less than in boiling.
Toasting	10–30 per cent of thiamine.

COOKING
ORGANIC

10

QUESTIONS

& ANSWERS

Q What are the alternatives to steaming or boiling frozen peas?

A *Whatever you do, you want to ensure that the peas are cooked for only a few minutes, in a tiny amount of water. As soon as they become bright green, turn off the heat and serve. Peas can be tossed in orange juice and served with toasted almonds, or drizzled with olive oil and garlic. Add some finely chopped chillies to the cooking water for extra zing. Peas are also delicious when mixed with a mint pesto made from roughly chopped mint leaves, organic olive oil and a little orange juice.*

Q If organic food is grown in compost, isn't there a risk of getting food poisoning? Should I cook the food for longer?

A *Composts present very little risk of food poisoning because of their balance of micro-organisms (see page 67), which destroy unhealthy bacteria and other infectious agents. All organic food should be washed carefully, but peeling and overcooking are not necessary.*

Q Do organic eggs need to be hard-boiled to prevent salmonella?

A *Conventional hens and, therefore, eggs hold a great risk of salmonella – that is why health experts recommend hard-boiling them, to ensure that any traces of the disease are killed. This is also why raw eggs and egg products are not recommended for pregnant women, children and the elderly. Organic eggs (see page 18) do not hold this risk, although it is sensible to avoid anything that is raw or lightly cooked during pregnancy because of the risk of contamination during transit.*

Q Can I juice all of my servings of fruit and vegetables, instead of eating them whole?

A *The nutrients found in fresh fruit and vegetables are also found in freshly squeezed juices, but it is not a good idea to rely on juices too heavily. They are a concentrated source of natural sugars, which can play havoc with your blood-sugar levels. Furthermore, they need to be drunk straight after juicing to provide the most nutrients. And juices do not contain plant fibre, which is an essential part of a healthy diet.*

Q How can I give roasted vegetables flavour?

A The natural flavour of vegetables will be brought out by the roasting process. The secret is to ensure that the oven is hot and that you do not overcook them. Roasted vegetables should be crisp, firm and brightly coloured. Before roasting, try tossing the vegetables in flavoured olive oil; garlic, herbs, organic sea salt and balsamic vinegar are another good choice; or go fruity, using freshly squeezed orange juice and zest, plus a little olive oil. Turn them often, and before serving toss in any juice that has drained out.

Q It seems a bit boring to steam all of my fruit and vegetables. What about cakes and other desserts? Are they off the menu?

A Absolutely not. It is perfectly possible to create delicious home-baked organic goods. As long as all of your ingredients are natural and organic, and you do not rely too heavily on sugar or salt, you can create healthy baked desserts with little effort. Try an organic rhubarb soufflé or a more traditional blackberry and apple crumble.

Q What is the best way to freeze fresh organic fruit and vegetables?

A Most fruit and vegetables can be frozen whole. Spread them out on a clean baking tray and put them straight into your freezer until they are solid. Seal them in bags or tubs until required. Some vegetables (such as peas and beans) are better blanched before being frozen (see page 85). Beware: although the nutritional content of frozen fruit and vegetables is often higher than that of fresh produce, the texture may be compromised, so use frozen produce in stews and soups.

Q Can you suggest a tasty dessert made from fresh organic fruit?

A There is nothing better than a good fruit salad. Chop as many different types of organic fruit as you can find into a bowl. Dribble with organic lemon juice to prevent browning. Add half a mug of fresh organic mango or orange juice, and the grated peel of an organic orange. Add two tablespoons of organic maple syrup, and toss the fruit in the sauce. Fresh mint makes a good, nutritious garnish. For a variation, add dried apricots or mango slices to the sauce 20 minutes before tossing with the fresh fruit. A sprinkling of cinnamon can add extra flavour.

Q Why is it still important to wash organic fruit and vegetables if pesticides haven't been used?

A There are a number of reasons. First of all, it will have passed through many hands, all of which have the potential to introduce bacteria, viruses or other micro-organisms to the food. Secondly, even organic soil is not sterile, and you will need to remove anything problematic before eating. Finally, pollution, 'acid' rain and other environmental by-products, as well as bird or animal droppings and insects, can make their way onto your produce in even the most natural environment. So wash all produce carefully.

Q My children won't eat vegetables. Is there an easy way to cook them that will make a difference?

A You can begin by disguising vegetables in nutritious pasta sauces, stews and soups. But all children need to learn to enjoy vegetables as part of a healthy diet, so it's important that they recognise and like them. Ask them to help with the preparation and encourage them to choose which vegetables will be served at each meal. Empowerment is a great tool for children! Try vegetables raw, stir-fried, sautéed, baked, roasted, smothered in sauce – whatever goes. You'll soon find something that appeals to your children.

7 ORGANIC FOR CHILDREN

CHAPTER

Going organic is an essential move for any adult who cares about health and the environment. However, the health implications of choosing anything other than organic for children can be very serious in the long term. Only now are we becoming aware of the problems associated with the modern diet, and while there are undoubtedly serious short-term effects (see box), the long-term prospects of living in our chemical environment may be nothing short of disastrous.

From the very first moments of conception right through to adulthood children are growing and developing. Everything that goes into or onto their bodies will play a part in their overall health, both now and in the future. Because they are smaller and their body systems are less mature, children are more susceptible to chemicals than adults. They have a greater need for nutrients, to ensure normal development and health, and need to build up a strong immunity to cope with the ever-increasing number of superbugs and viruses – particularly in the face of the additional demands placed on their bodies as children.

Adopting an organic lifestyle makes sense for every parent. It is no coincidence that an increased number of miscarriages and stillbirths, plus cancers, birth defects, heart diseases, allergies and auto-immune

Involve your children in growing organic vegetables, or plan a family outing to an organic farm, where you can pick your own fruit and vegetables.

92

conditions in children, has coincided with the expansion of the processed, convenience-food market based on intensively farmed foods. Children need good, nutritious, fresh food, and they need an environment that is as free from chemicals as possible. From the moment a parent makes the decision to have a baby, the emphasis should be on reducing the number of toxins in food and in products used in the home. The best and safest way to do this is to go organic.

WHY ORGANIC?

PRECONCEPTION AND PREGNANCY: there are now literally hundreds of studies showing a link between maternal eating habits and environmental factors, such as smoking, on the health of an unborn child. A lack of key nutrients and a preponderance of toxins can have an effect on everything from birth weight, IQ, immunity and future fertility through to allergies, cancers, hyperactivity, sleep disorders and normal growth patterns. Choosing organic during preconception and pregnancy means ensuring a good supply of these essential nutrients, as well as cutting down on harmful toxins.

GM-FREE FOODS (see pages 30–31): organic foods contain no GMOs, which could cause fatal allergies, antibiotic resistance and possibly even genetic damage.

TOXIN-FREE PRODUCTS: organic foods and other products are free from toxic chemicals, which can have a serious impact on health (see pages 34–35). Organic food does not contain artificial additives and preservatives, flavourings, sugars, colourings and sweeteners.

REDUCING FOOD POISONING: conventionally produced food is rife with food-borne illnesses (see pages 27 and 29). Children are particularly susceptible to these infections, which may even cause death.

ESTABLISHING GOOD EATING HABITS: when children become accustomed to eating nutritious organic food, as opposed to conventional junk food, good eating habits are established, which will help to keep them healthy in the present and in turn to protect their future.

UNDERSTANDING THE ENVIRONMENT: going organic teaches our children about the slow food movement. This term refers to the way in which due care and attention are paid to production in organic farming (rather than to quickly produced foods for maximum yield and profit). This encourages a responsible approach to consumption. Future generations will undoubtedly depend upon a more environmentally friendly way of life.

IMMUNITY: your child's immunity is his first and last defence against disease. Consuming even low levels of antibiotics over a period of time can interfere with your child's immune system, making them more susceptible to colds and other infections. Worse still, if life-saving antibiotics are then required, they will be less effective and perhaps even ineffective. Going organic will help to build up a strong immune system, which is essential for life.

ORGANIC FOR HEALTH

Children today eat a fairly unvaried diet, based on processed, kid-friendly food. But even children who are eating a good diet, based on wholefoods, fresh fruit and vegetables that are farmed conventionally, may be heading for trouble. Governments around the world have set safe limits for pesticides and other toxic chemicals; however, what may be an acceptable level for a fully grown man will certainly not be safe for a child. All the problems associated with conventionally grown food are relevant to children. In fact, their impact is intensified, because their bodies are smaller, their systems less mature, their organs less developed and they tend to eat much the same types of foods, which means that their intake of one or a group of pesticides can be much higher than average. For example, the average child tends to eat plenty of apples, bananas, oranges and pears, all of which are heavily sprayed. Another popular choice is sweetcorn, which is now genetically modified. And children are the biggest milk drinkers of any age group – and this adds the risks associated with BST, antibiotics, GMOs and hormones.

FOOD AND CHILDREN

What your child eats is matter of considerable concern:

🪰 Organic food is by nature less likely to cause overweight, because it is based on whole, natural, unrefined ingredients. Obesity has serious health risks, including heart disease. In the US 21 per cent of children are considered obese.

🪰 A 1995 study revealed that pupils showed a rise of 1–15 IQ points after beginning a programme that eliminated sugar and refined foods.

🪰 Behaviour, learning and health problems were compared in boys with high and low intakes of essential fatty acids (not present in the average child's non-organic diet). More behavioural problems were found in those with low omega-3 fatty acid intakes, and more learning and health problems in those with lower omega-6 intakes.

🪰 It is estimated that 3–4 per cent of children in primary school have severe iron-deficiency anaemia. Low blood iron levels can translate to poor school performance and are linked to decreased attention and concentration, irritability, low IQ tests (especially in vocabulary), perceptual difficulties and underachievement.

🪰 Children who are deficient in just one or two key nutrients can show symptoms that will affect both their development and school work.

🪰 A joint report by the World Cancer Research Fund (WCRF) and the American Institute for Cancer Research (AICR) claims that 30–40 per cent of cancers may be caused by dietary factors. Studies show that simply adding fruit and vegetables to your diet can reduce your risk of cancer by 20 per cent. Make those organic, and your child will be that much better off.

🪰 Processed foods contain a huge number of chemicals, the effects of which are only just beginning to be understood. Many additives have now been banned, but some (particularly tartrazine or E102) have been linked to hyperactivity in children, allergies, asthma, migraines and even cancer.

'GENDER-BENDER' CHEMICALS

And there's more. Conventionally farmed foods use numerous chemicals that can interfere with our normal body functioning. Take the 'gender-bender' chemicals, for example: organochlorines (more than 11,000 different ones are being used today, in products that range from pesticides and plastics to dental fillings, toothpaste and mouthwash) can mimic the effect of natural substances such as oestrogen that play a key role in our reproductive system. These hormone disrupters are believed to cause birth defects, falling sperm counts, infertility and other reproductive problems (including early puberty and menopause), as well as decreasing resistance to disease by suppressing our immune systems.

DISPOSABLE NAPPIES

There are many concerns that the chemicals used in the manufacture of disposable nappies can leach into your baby's skin, causing problems with fertility, among other things. A recent study also showed that disposable nappies heat the genital area to an unacceptable level, potentially damaging fertility and acting as a breeding ground for infection.

And there are other issues: disposable nappies create more than 800,000 ton(ne)s of rubbish, costing an estimated £40m a year to collect and dispose of in landfill sites. More than seven million trees are cut down to make nappies each year, and a great deal of pollution is created both by their production and their disposal. Toxic organochlorines, such as dioxins, are also created in the production of disposables, in both wood pulp and plastics manufacture.

Ideally, use reusable unbleached cotton-and-wool organic nappies, in order to reduce the considerable risks (see page 100) both to your baby and to the environment. Although they may be expensive in terms of initial outlay, they will be much cheaper in the long run.

A healthy organic diet is one of the most important things you can do to ensure your child's good health. But try not to force the issue – making mealtimes fun can go a long way towards ensuring a healthy attitude towards food.

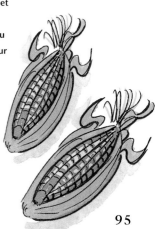

CREATING HEALTHY HABITS

Raising a child on fresh, healthy organic food is not difficult. Whether you choose to breastfeed or bottlefeed, make your own babyfoods or buy them, eat a vegetarian diet or traditional fare, there are organic options. And where children are concerned, organic is definitely best.

One of the most difficult things facing parents today is the junk-food culture. It is difficult to persuade a savvy six-year-old that organic beansprouts are more fun than a McDonald's, but if your child has been brought up on a healthy organic diet from day one, he will be much more likely to adopt eating habits that will stand him in good stead for the rest of his life. And organic food does not have to be boring – fresh, whole foods can be just as much fun as their conventional equivalents, and your child will learn to appreciate the taste of food that is not smothered in additives and colourings. In fact, children who have been given organic food from the beginning often find conventionally produced food either bland or too strongly flavoured. There is no reason why you cannot make your own healthy organic chips (see page 87); and organic sausages and mash look just the same as conventional varieties, but without any of the risks. In the end a hungry child will eat whatever is on offer, and the rewards are well worth the effort required.

ORGANIC FROM THE BEGINNING

◆ There is no question that breast is best. Even breastmilk is known to contain environmental toxins, so who knows what cows fed on hormones, GM feed, antibiotics and heavily sprayed feed will produce? If you have to bottlefeed, choose organic milk, to avoid the risks associated with cow's milk (see pages 42–43).

◆ Babies should never be weaned before four or five months of age, and some experts now recommend waiting for up to nine months before beginning solids. Six months is a good age to start with a little table food – some organic rice, a few fruit and vegetables, for example – but leave it longer if you can, particularly if there are allergies of any nature in your family. Introducing foods too early can cause allergies in susceptible children, largely by overloading their system. This is why organic food is important, as it reduces pressure on your baby's body.

Breastfeeding is undoubtedly the best way to feed your baby, and it's a good way to establish a close relationship. But if you can't, or dislike the thought of nursing, choose an organic formula, which is free of chemicals that could harm your baby.

✦ Preparing your own babyfood is the cheapest, safest way to feed your baby. Choose a wide variety of organic fruit, vegetables and rice, adding a little organic meat, such as chicken, when your baby is ready. Babyfood can be puréed and frozen in ice-cube trays to be defrosted as required. As children become older you can educate their palates by introducing all sorts of delicious herbs and vegetables. Don't hesitate to mix fruit and vegetables: peas and pears go well together, as do carrots and apricots.

✦ Organic jarred babyfood is perfect for travelling, but avoid depending on it too much. It tends to be bland and expensive, and you may find yourself with a baby who will not eat anything that doesn't come in a jar.

✦ As your child grows older, continue to serve organic food, focusing on unrefined grains, rice, fruit, vegetables, lean meat and pulses. Nutritious stews, casseroles and soups are a good way to incorporate a wide variety of different foods

in one meal. If time is at a premium, get your child used to eating stir-fries, organic pastas with vegetable sauces and fresh, crunchy salads. Encourage your children to help with the preparation – there are very few children who won't eat what they have made themselves, and rebellion is usually short-lived if you explain why you are making the changes.

Children who are encouraged to take an interest in cooking and food preparation are much more likely to show a healthy interest in food. They're also less likely to decline something they've made themselves!

✦ Fill your fruit bowl with a variety of organic produce and keep crudités to hand, as well as organic ricecakes, cheese, popcorn, cereals and toast, biscuits for treats and good-quality yoghurts and dried fruit.

✦ Ensure that the organic alternatives are fun. The occasional organic lemonade won't be too problematic, if the rest of your child's diet is healthy. Or encourage children to make their own fizzy drinks with organic juice and carbonated water. Organic hamburgers can be made from good-quality organic meat and then grilled rather than fried. Buy an organic pizza base and ask children to make their own toppings, offering lots of vegetables and organic cheese.

✦ Most importantly, teach your children about food and healthy eating. If they understand *why* they eat what they do, they will learn to make the right choices as they grow into adults.

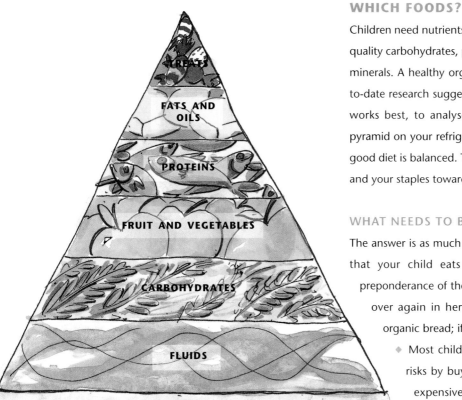

WHICH FOODS?

Children need nutrients in order to grow. That means plenty of good-quality carbohydrates, protein, healthy fats, water, fibre, vitamins and minerals. A healthy organic diet will provide just that. The most up-to-date research suggests that a pyramid structure (see diagram left) works best, to analyse how your diet should be set up. Pin the pyramid on your refrigerator so that the whole family can see how a good diet is balanced. The items you should eat least of are at the top and your staples towards the bottom.

WHAT NEEDS TO BE ORGANIC?

The answer is as much as you can afford, based on the types of food that your child eats most of. What you want to avoid is a preponderance of the same types of chemicals appearing over and over again in her diet. So if she is a big toast eater, choose organic bread; if she loves apple juice, buy organic.

◆ Most children drink a great deal of milk, so reduce the risks by buying organic (which is not substantially more expensive), particularly if they are also fond of cheese and yoghurt.

◆ Meat, eggs and root vegetables are most likely to contain dangerous chemicals that are the result of intensive farming, so it is wise to play safe with these particular foods. Remember that children do not need a lot of meat and can get protein from other sources.

◆ Grains are now particularly in the spotlight, because they are so heavily sprayed and absorb far more dangerous chemicals than some other foods. Given that most children eat toast, cereal, pasta and sandwiches regularly, it really does make sense to buy organic varieties of these foods.

THE FOOD PYRAMID

TREATS: sweets, cakes, biscuits, fast food (not to be eaten on a daily basis).

FATS AND OILS: includes butter, olive oil, unhydrogenated margarines, seed and nut oils (use sparingly).

PROTEINS: includes very lean meat, fish, poultry, cheese, yoghurt, nuts, soya products (including tofu), pulses such as lentils, and seeds (3–5 servings a day).

FRUIT AND VEGETABLES: includes their juices (anything goes); the more colourful the vegetable, the more nutritious it tends to be (5–7 servings a day).

CARBOHYDRATES: anything wholegrain or unrefined, including pasta, bread, brown rice, grains (such as rye, barley, corn and buckwheat), pulses, potatoes and wholegrain, sugar-free cereals (4–9 servings a day).

FLUIDS: water is the most important.

◆ With all the problems that are associated with genetic modification, it is always safest to buy organic soya, which you know does not contain GM ingredients.

◆ Organic snacks are a much better bet than non-organic, because of the potential risks from GM ingredients (see pages 30–31), which are found in so many traditional snacks.

◆ If you eat too many fresh products to buy all-organic, then wash everything very carefully or peel it. There are now special detergents that remove waxes, pesticides and other substances sprayed on the skin of fruit and vegetables, which can help to limit the damage caused by these substances.

◆ Remember that organic food is not as expensive as you may think. If you use it as a supplement to your ordinary shopping, you may notice a difference. However, cutting out all junk food and focusing on a little meat, plenty of fruit and vegetables, some good pasta and bread, rice, pulses and dairy foods can be much cheaper than buying a trolley-load of convenience offerings.

◆ If your child is a tinned-food junkie, it is worth buying the organic options. Baked beans and soups may contain a wide variety of nasty ingredients, and what should be nutritious ends up being nothing more than a tinful of chemicals.

◆ Consider buying organic produce from a local greengrocer. It tends to be cheaper and the food is fresher. Another good option is an organic delivery service (see pages 60–61).

◆ Choose organic fruit and vegetables that are in season. They are always much cheaper than imported goods.

◆ Use your freezer! If organic beans are on special offer in the supermarket, then buy lots and freeze them.

Make food fun! Grow it, choose it and cook it together, and food will have pleasurable associations that will last throughout your child's lifetime.

ORGANIC
FOR
CHILDREN

QUESTIONS
& ANSWERS

Q Do I need to buy organic toothpaste for my children, or is a 'natural' toothpaste all right?

A *Although natural toothpastes are undoubtedly better for you than the average supermarket brand, they can still contain a variety of chemicals, including organochlorines, artificial sweeteners, colourings and fluoride. Many conventional brands of toothpaste also contain very high levels of fluoride, which can be toxic if taken in excess. Fluoride toothpaste contains 1,000 parts fluoride per million – enough to kill an 8kg/17½lb child if a whole 200ml/7fl oz tube is taken orally. Choose organic, if you can.*

Q Do I need to use organic shampoos and body lotions for my baby?

A *Organic body products are much safer than the conventional alternatives, and given that you will be using them directly on your baby's skin, which absorbs the toxins or nutrition in anything that you apply, then organic is the best option. Organic shampoos and creams are natural and as toxin-free as possible. You will know that whatever goes into your baby's body will do no harm.*

Q Are organic disposable nappies environmentally friendly?

A *Organic disposable nappies are not yet widely available, but they have the same benefits as any organic product, which means that they cause little or no harm to the environment. Your best bet, however, is to use reusable unbleached cotton-and-wool organic nappies. According to the Women's Environmental Network, you will be protecting your baby from gels, glues, chlorine bleach, plastics, formaldehyde, dyes, artificial perfumes, chemical lotions and other toxins that are found in both plastic and paper disposable nappies.*

Q My daughter has always been a fussy eater and has never touched anything that isn't processed and refined. Why does she look so healthy?

A *Don't be fooled. Many children seem to exist on nothing more than crisps and spaghetti hoops, but the damage is being done well below the surface. Children who eat badly are more likely to suffer from attention problems, obesity, cancer, osteoporosis and even fertility problems as adults. Your daughter's immune system will be impaired, and the foundation of her body – her organs, bones and even blood – will not have received the nutrients they need to mature properly.*

Q I don't have much time to cook, so how can I provide a healthy organic diet for my children?

A *It takes only 20 minutes to chop and prepare a nutritious stir-fry, and, when you do have time, you can cook in advance, freezing soups, casseroles and pasta dishes for busy periods. There are plenty of organic convenience foods now on the market, such as pastas and pizzas; add some extra vegetables, serve with a glass of organic juice, offer an organic yoghurt with honey and dried fruit for dessert – and you have a well-balanced organic meal. Organic baked potatoes are another easy, quick choice.*

Q My child won't eat vegetables or fruit. How can I get him to change?

A *Buy organic! They taste much better, which will convert many children. And if you have to, get sneaky: add organic vegetables to pasta sauces, soups and pizzas. Use a juicer to make delicious blends of vegetable and fruit juices. Encourage him to choose combinations and to become involved in the process. Continue to offer fruit and vegetables at every meal, but don't make a fuss if he doesn't eat them. He will soon come round, particularly if there is no alternative. Explain why these foods are so important, and ask him to help plan your menus.*

Q Is organic bedding necessary?

A *It helps. Many children's sheets, pillows and duvet covers have been treated with flame-retardant chemicals (linked to cot death), formaldehyde, strong bleaches, dyes and other chemicals. Given that children spend so much time in bed, then a natural, chemical-free environment is a much healthier option. Organic bedding is untreated and conforms to international organic standards, which means that you will be helping to protect the environment.*

Q Should I buy organic formula for my baby?

A *Yes, it is not much more expensive than conventional brands, and it is an important choice to make if you decide to bottlefeed, largely because of the problems associated with the milk industry. When you think of the risks associated with BST, antibiotics, GMOs and hormones, you have a real problem on your hands, and buying organic is the answer.*

Q Are 'sugar-free' products better than products containing organic sugar?

A *It depends on the product! Check the label to ensure that it really is sugar-free. Many products claiming to be sugarless contain chemical sweeteners, such as aspartame (see page 46). If you had to choose between a sugar-free and an organic fruit drink, for example, the organic brand would be more likely to contain fewer chemicals, additives or colourings. However, too much sugar is unhealthy, so you should go with the foods and drinks that are closest to nature: that is, pure and unadulterated.*

Q I can't afford to buy organic for my children, so what should I do?

A *First of all, cut out everything from your shopping list that isn't necessary (biscuits, ready prepared meals, soft drinks, chocolates, crisps, for example). You'll find that removing these items from your shopping list cuts the total bill dramatically. Then buy everything that your children eat (or should eat) on a daily basis in organic form. If you eat a lot of meat, consider choosing some vegetable proteins instead, such as tofu, pulses and grains. Most consumers find that eating organic isn't much more expensive if they focus on health rather than treats.*

101

8 ORGANIC IN THE HOME

There are literally hundreds of reasons why it makes sense to go organic in your home. The health implications are obvious: toxic chemicals are linked to many health problems, some of them more sinister than others. Many organic products are not only devoid of toxic chemicals, but have positive health benefits. Hemp, for example, is now used in many household products and clothing and is a rich source of essential fatty acids, which can be absorbed through the skin. Other organic products contain essential oils, which have therapeutic benefits too.

CHEMICAL SENSITIVITY

A report entitled 'Multiple Chemical Sensitivity Recognition' was recently published by the British Society for Allergy, Environmental and Nutritional Medicine. It urged the government to tighten the regulations concerning chemical use, imposing stricter controls on the authorisation of new chemicals and requiring the removal of persistent chemicals from food. The authors found that exposure to chemicals can not only cause allergies and fatigue, but can lead to a condition called 'multiple chemical sensitivity', which involves developing a severe allergy to chemicals in everyday products. Allergies are still not fully understood, but we do know that they represent a profound breakdown in the immune response, which recognises ordinary substances as invaders. Research published by the European Chemicals Bureau shows that only 14 per cent of the most heavily used chemicals have a full set of basic safety data publicly available. In other words, we do not know the long-term effects of the majority of chemicals that we use on a daily basis.

If you have a highly toxic environment, you may be undoing some of the benefits of eating well. Taking that one step further, it's possible to enhance a good diet by ensuring that you cut down on toxins in your environment. That means looking carefully at cleaning products, carpeting, paint, furnishings and even bedding. You don't have to make changes overnight – simply switch to safer alternatives when it's time to renew or replace household items.

Consider the wider picture. The chemicals we use in our home play havoc with the environment and affect all forms of wildlife.

CHOOSING HOUSEHOLD PRODUCTS

Organic products are required to conform to environmental criteria (protecting wildlife, encouraging recycling, using less energy and more natural renewable resources and reducing pollution). Their manufacturers also encourage fair trade with developing countries, support a healthier farming system, actively lobby against genetic modification and help to preserve both the local countryside and the planet in general.

When shopping for household products, remember the following salient points:

◆ The term 'natural' has very little meaning. By law, only a small percentage of ingredients need to be natural for this term to be used on the label.

◆ Choose organic if you have the choice – you know exactly what you are getting.

◆ Read the label. If you recognise the majority of the ingredients (lemon juice, bicarbonate of soda, hydrogen peroxide or washing soda, for example), the product is a much safer option. If it reads like a chemistry textbook, give it a miss.

◆ A number of independent third-party organisations develop standards and guidelines for green products and services. Look out for their kite-marks on products.

◆ Choose products with minimal (and recyclable) packaging.

◆ Better still, buy the ingredients to make your own household products (see pages 104–105). This is cheaper and much healthier for you, your family and the environment.

HAZARDOUS HOUSEHOLD CHEMICALS

Some products are not only toxic, but dangerous. Some 12 per cent of all calls to poison-control centres are the result of household cleaning products, which contain chemicals that are poisonous, corrosive, flammable and/or chemically reactive. The worst offenders in this category include:

◆ car fluids (such as antifreeze, screen wash, brake fluid, battery fluid)
◆ disinfectants
◆ household cleaners
◆ paint products
◆ pesticides

◆ personal-hygiene products (such as deodorants, bubble bath)
◆ pet-care products
◆ photographic chemicals
◆ polishes (such as furniture and floor polish)
◆ swimming-pool chemicals

CLEANING PRODUCTS

Here are some useful alternatives to manufactured cleaning products. They are not only safer and far less toxic, but work extremely well.

AIR FRESHENER Simmer cinnamon and cloves; use organic aromatherapy oils in water and spritz using a pump spray; add a few drops of organic tea-tree and lemon essential oils to some bicarbonate of soda, then sprinkle on your carpets and vacuum up.

ALUMINIUM SPOT REMOVER 2 tbsp cream of tartar in 1l/1¾pt hot water.

ANT POWDER Strew pennyroyal or mint to deter them. Growing mints or tansy near their entrance will help. Non-drying sticky bands are an effective preventative barrier.

BLEACH Borax, washing soda (available in liquid form) or hydrogen peroxide.

BRASS POLISH Worcestershire sauce.

CHROME POLISH Apple cider vinegar; then polish with organic baby oil.

CLEANER (*general household*) Mix ¼ cup bicarbonate of soda with organic liquid-soap solution and ¼ cup vinegar, then add 6 drops organic tea-tree oil and 6 drops lemon essential oil; or try 1l/1¾pt hot water, 1 tsp organic vegetable oil-based soap/detergent, 1 tsp borax and 2 tbsp vinegar.

COCKROACH REPELLENT Chopped bay leaves and cucumber skins.

COFFEE-CUP STAIN REMOVER Moist salt.

COFFEE-POT STAIN REMOVER Vinegar.

COPPER CLEANER Lemon juice and salt.

DISH DETERGENT Organic liquid detergent mixed with ½ cup bicarbonate of soda.

DRAIN CLEANER Plunger, followed by ½ cup baking soda mixed with ½ cup vinegar and 2l/3½pt boiling water.

FURNITURE POLISH 1 tbsp organic lemon essential oil in 600ml/1pt organic mineral oil or olive oil.

INK-SPOT REMOVER Cold water with 1 tbsp cream of tartar and 1 tbsp lemon juice.

LAUNDRY DETERGENT Use laundry soap in place of detergents, with ½ cup washing soda as a softener; use eco-friendly detergents with no added bleaches, phosphates or softeners.

LAUNDRY PRE-SOAK Make a paste of washing soda and water, then apply to spots.

LINOLEUM FLOOR CLEANER 1 cup white vinegar and 2l/3½pt water; add a few drops of organic lemon essential oil for its scent and 4 drops tea-tree oil for its antibacterial/antiviral properties.

MILDEW REMOVER Equal parts of vinegar and salt.

MOSQUITO REPELLENT Burn citronella candles.

MOTH REPELLENT Cedar chips or dried lavender flowers enclosed in cotton sachets.

MULTI-PURPOSE CLEANER Mix ½ cup ammonia, ⅓ cup vinegar, ¼ cup baking soda in 1l/1¾pt warm water.

OIL-STAIN REMOVER White chalk rubbed into the stain before laundering.

OVEN CLEANER 2 tbsp liquid organic soap, 2 tsp borax and warm water; or try a paste of salt, bicarbonate of soda and water: leave for 20 minutes, then scrub.

PET-ODOUR REMOVER Cider vinegar sprinkled over the area.

PORCELAIN CLEANER Make a paste of bicarbonate of soda and water: let it set, then rub clean and rinse.

REFRIGERATOR DEODORISER Leave an open box of bicarbonate of soda with 2 drops each of organic lemon and tea-tree essential oils permanently in the refrigerator.

RUG/CARPET CLEANER Soda water; or mix 600ml/1pt warm water, 1 tsp organic liquid soap, 1 tsp borax and a splash of vinegar: apply with a damp cloth to the carpet and rub gently; blot and vacuum normally when dry.

RUST REMOVAL (clothing) Lemon juice and salt rubbed into the stain, then put in the sunlight to bleach.

SCORCH-MARK REMOVAL Grated onion.

SCOURING POWDER Bicarbonate of soda.

SILVER POLISH 600ml/1pt warm water with 1 tbsp bicarbonate of soda and 1 tbsp salt: line your sink with aluminium foil and soak.

SLUG AND SNAIL REPELLENT Onion and marigold plants.

SPOT REMOVER Soda water, lemon juice or salt.

STAINLESS-STEEL POLISH Organic mineral oil or olive oil.

TOILET-BOWL CLEANER Make a paste of borax and lemon juice: let it sit for 20 minutes, then scrub the toilet with a bowl brush; let 1 cup borax sit in the bowl overnight.

TUB AND TILE CLEANER ¼ cup baking soda, ½ cup white vinegar, 2 drops organic lemon essential oil, 2 drops tea-tree oil and warm water.

WATER SOFTENER ¼ cup vinegar.

WINDOW CLEANER ½ cup vinegar in 1l/1¾pt warm water; add 1 drop of organic lemon essential oil if you want a lemony smell.

WINE-STAIN REMOVER Salt.

WOOD POLISH 3 parts olive oil to 1 part white vinegar; almond or olive oil (interior unvarnished wood only).

PERSONAL HYGIENE

Whatever you put on your body is absorbed by your skin and can either enhance your health or increase your chemical load. Choosing organic personal-hygiene products is not only important for children, but also for women in particular, who take in twice their body weight in toxic chemicals during their lifetime, compared to men's consumption of half their body weight. Women are also more likely to come into contact with household chemicals, which lie at the root of hormonal imbalances, causing conditions such as PMS, fertility problems and early puberty, as well as many menopausal symptoms.

So look at the labels very carefully. If it is not practical to purchase all-organic products, go for natural ingredients, such as essential oils, herbs, olive oil, rose water and sea salts.

WHAT TO LOOK OUT FOR

The label tells the whole story. Sodium laureth sulfate, methylparaben, propylparaben, DEA (diethanolamine), TEA (triethanolamine), PEG (polyethylene glycol), quaternium-15, propylene glycol, animal products and other toxic chemicals are the main ingredients in most body-care products. Watch out for companies using the word 'organic' – some are adding just one or two organic ingredients to an otherwise toxic cocktail, or are referring to the chemical term 'organic' (as in 'organic chemistry'). A genuinely organic product will not contain any of the above chemicals and will normally be certified or recommended by one of the organic governing bodies (see pages 16 and 116–119). All organic products should be 100 per cent cruelty-free.

Many of the personal products we choose contain chemicals that can damage our health and that of the environment. Some of the new organic products use natural ingredients that can complement a healthy lifestyle.

106

WHAT ARE THE ALTERNATIVES?

If you cannot find, or cannot afford to purchase, all-organic products, then why not look in your store cupboard for substitutes? There are many food items that can successfully be used on the body, and natural substitutes for other items of personal hygiene. Here are some ideas that are worth trying out. The rest is up to you.

MOISTURISER Organic olive oil is an excellent whole-body moisturiser. Pour a few tablespoons into the bath after you have been soaking, then dry off normally; or use it as a conventional moisturiser. Organic cocoa butter and coconut oil, or any of the natural organic oils used in aromatherapy (such as grapeseed, almond and peach kernel), are other good choices. Or rub the skin of an organic avocado on your face and body, then rinse and pat dry.

SHAMPOO AND CONDITIONER Choose a good-quality eco-friendly shampoo as a base and add your own ingredients. Any organic essential oil will scent your hair, as well as providing therapeutic benefits – one drop is all you need. Wash your hair in chamomile tea with some organic lemon juice to reduce oil build-up. Use olive oil as a natural conditioner: it rinses out well in warm water. If your hair is still greasy, rinse again with warm water and a drop of lemon juice. Mashed avocado or whipped organic eggs make a good intensive conditioner.

DEODORANT Always use deodorant rather than antiperspirant (see page 35). Deodorant stones are now available – they are made from crystal (natural mineral salts), without any harmful aluminium chlorohydrate, perfumes, emulsifiers or propellants. You wet the stone and rub it under your arm and it works by attacking the bacteria. Alternatively, blend one drop of organic tea-tree and one of lavender essential oil in olive oil, then rub liberally under your arms. This will disguise any odour and even prevent it, by killing bacterial overgrowth. Pat dry before dressing.

CLEANSER Rose water makes an excellent cleanser and toner and is safe for all skin types. Cucumber juice and cooled chamomile tea are other good choices. If your skin is slightly greasy, use rosemary tea, which acts as an astringent. Witch hazel is a good alternative, but dilute it carefully (at least half and half, depending on the sensitivity of your skin). Test it on the inside of your arm.

FEMININE PROTECTION Choose certified-organic cotton disposables (see page 35).

TOOTHPASTE Choose an organic or homeopathic brand, or brush with bicarbonate of soda blended with fresh organic lemon juice. If you are a mint-lover, crush in a little fresh organic peppermint.

DEPILATORY Natural beeswax strips are your safest bet. They do not contain chemicals and they are reusable.

AN ORGANIC HOUSEHOLD

What is even better than 'greening' your home? Going organic, of course. Here we look at some of the practical ways you can cut down on the chemicals in your house. Not all the alternatives are organic, but buy what you can, choosing recognised names from reputable companies (try organic mail-order companies, or the organic section of your health-food shop or supermarket).

More than 50,000 chemicals now appear in products widely available on supermarket shelves. And that does not even take into consideration the fact that furnishings, pet products, timber treatments, carpets, paints and other products contain even more. While one or more of these chemicals may be safe on their own, the US Environmental Protection Agency (EPA) has warned that when several chemicals are combined, this could cause problems 'at levels below thresholds presently known to cause adverse health effects'. Short-term exposure to these toxic cocktails can aggravate symptoms of fatigue, headaches, dizziness, nausea and skin irritation within hours of use. Long-term exposure has been linked to cancer, respiratory disease, immune-system suppression, birth defects and even genetic changes.

Some products, such as paint and wood treatments, are specialist ones, but it is worth looking at what is on offer if you plan to redecorate, for example, or if you have a new baby on the way and want to make your home as safe as possible.

Organic paints and other DIY products are now available in a wide range of colours and finishes. If it's time to redecorate, why not choose the healthy alternatives?

WHAT ARE THE ALTERNATIVES?

TOILET PAPER Choose recycled toilet paper that is either unbleached or treated with oxygen bleach, rather than dioxin-producing chlorine bleach. Some toilet papers are now labelled organic, which means that the trees used for their production meet organic standards.

CARPETS Choose products with organic cotton, wool or hemp, and no pesticides, dyes (biocides to deter mould) or stain protections. Conventional carpets can cause serious health problems: for example, adhesive 4-PC (4-phenylcyclohexane) and at least 31 chemicals such as styrene come from the SB latex backing used on 95 per cent of carpets. Styrene is a known toxin and a suspected carcinogen. Health complaints associated with carpets include neurological, central nervous system and respiratory problems. Multiple Chemical Sensitivity (MCS) and Environmental Illness (EI) are also on the increase. Volatile organic compounds (VOCs) and formaldehyde are often found in conventional carpets.

PAINTS Use latex (water-based), non-toxic paint instead of oil-based paint, which contains a high percentage of solvents that contribute to air pollution. Organic paints are much safer (see page 64). There are also organic paint thinners, made from natural ingredients. Both products emit only natural, pleasant fragrances.

BODY-CARE PRODUCTS See pages 106–107.

HOUSEHOLD CLEANING PRODUCTS See pages 104–105.

BEDDING AND CLOTHING Choose organic cotton or hemp, wherever possible. Synthetic fabrics (such as nylon or rayon) are by definition made by means of 'chemical synthesis'. Conventional cotton is produced with some 35 different pesticides and herbicides, and the cotton industry is responsible for 50 per cent of all chemicals used in the world for agricultural purposes. Organic cotton is grown without any manmade chemicals; only natural means, such as the Australian wasp, are used to control pests that land or feed on the cotton plants.

PET PRODUCTS Spraying your household or pet with flea killers or deterrents will undoubtedly affect your own health. These products are pesticides, and they affect the neurological systems of humans as well. So choose natural brands containing essential oils (such as tea tree) or herbs that are known to deter pests. Experiment with natural flea repellents (see also page 111) such as eucalyptus, citronella, cedarwood, pennyroyal and black walnut leaves. Vacuum your house and clean your pet's bedding frequently. Steam-cleaning, particularly using essential oils, kills adult fleas, the larvae and some eggs. Pyrethrin is an organically-approved pesticide in the US (it is not approved in the UK at present): watch out, though, as it is often mixed with more toxic ingredients.

TIMBER TREATMENTS AND OTHER DIY PRODUCTS These traditionally contain chemicals such as lindane (linked to breast cancer), insecticides, fungicides (TBTO and PCP, an organochlorine fungicide, see page 95) and colouring. Organic products are now available, or choose brands that use natural products such as beeswax, citrus oil or tung oil as a sealant, and borax for preventing fungi and insects.

FURNITURE Choose products that are free of toxic glues, formaldehyde and fibreboard. This last is made from wood fibres or particles bonded together with the synthetic resin urea-formaldehyde, from which fumes leak for years. Make sure that your products are treated only with natural chemicals, such as beeswax and borax.

ORGANIC IN THE HOME

10

QUESTIONS
& ANSWERS

Q Is there such a thing as an organic light bulb?

A Strictly speaking no, but you will be doing your part for the environment by choosing energy-saving bulbs. For all the light energy produced from the ordinary light bulb, 30 times as much is wasted in the conversion of the locked-up coal energy into electricity. Low-energy fluorescent light bulbs or tubes use only one-fifth of the electricity of ordinary incandescent light bulbs. It has been estimated that each low-energy light source saves the atmosphere from receiving almost 1 ton(ne) of carbon dioxide – and they last about five times as long as ordinary bulbs.

Q What organic body-care products would you recommend for a baby?

A If you can buy organic products, go ahead and use them, but remember that babies do not need moisturisers, nappy creams, bubble baths or powders. Add a drop of organic lavender essential oil to the bath to kill unhealthy bacteria, and use organic soap and shampoo sparingly. Most babies can be washed squeaky-clean in warm water alone. If your baby's skin is dry, give her a massage with some warmed organic almond or olive oil to nourish her without causing the toxic side-effects of conventional moisturisers.

Q Why do organic products have to be recyclable?

A One of the principles of organic agriculture and processing is to work, as far as possible, with materials and substances that can be reused or recycled, either on the farm or elsewhere. That means recycling kitchen waste in the form of compost; recycling paper, metals and glass; and choosing products that use recycled ingredients or packaging.

Q Is there such a product as organic hairspray?

A Most hairsprays are nothing more than chemical glues, but there are new products on the market (in pump sprays, of course) that contain natural ingredients such as herbs and essential oils. If you can find an organic brand, then you are lucky. Second best is an environmentally friendly brand that does not contain anything but natural resins.

Q What is an eco-ball?

A *An eco-ball is a chemical-free laundry ball that replaces all soaps and detergents. It normally lasts for about 750 washes, and works by producing ionised oxygen, which activates the water molecules so that they penetrate clothing fibres and lift dirt away. Eco-balls are hypo-allergenic, antibacterial and fragrance-free, leaving no residues. They are also believed to save water and electricity. While not strictly organic, they are an excellent alternative to conventional and even 'green' laundry detergents.*

Q Can I buy an organic water filter?

A *Household 'appliances' are not usually certified organic because they do not contain agricultural ingredients. However, a good water filter is essential in order to remove pollutants such as pesticides, herbicides and nitrate residues from farming, heavy metals, oestrogen, fluoride and chlorine. Ask your local organic supplier if they can recommend a good one.*

Q I have a real problem with moths in my house. Is there an organic solution I could try?

A *There are now organic mothballs on the market, which contain no pesticides or other chemicals that will damage your health. Conventional mothballs contain a poison called paradichlorobenzene. If you cannot find organic alternatives, use organic cedarwood or lavender essential oil or camphor. They can be soaked into a piece of muslin (or organic cotton) and placed strategically around your home.*

Q What is all the fuss about hemp?

A *Hemp is a natural beauty product: the seeds comprise 30 per cent oils, the highest natural source of linoleic and linolenic acids (the compounds responsible for the lustre of skin, hair and eyes), plus 25 per cent protein (almost as much as soya beans – in fact they are far higher in fibre and certain vitamins and minerals). Hemp does not require pesticides to grow and is one of the earth's primary renewable resources: it can be cultivated in as little as 100 days and can yield four times more paper than trees over a 20-year period. Well worth a try.*

Q How can I deter fleas and ticks on my pets?

A *Scatter pine needles, fennel, rye or rosemary on your pet's bed, and spritz your carpet and upholstery regularly with organic tea-tree essential oil diluted in a little water. You can also feed your pet brewer's yeast, vitamin B or garlic tablets, and spritz its body with two drops of tea-tree oil diluted in a cup of warm water, making sure that you avoid its eyes while doing this.*

Q My supermarket sells toilet paper that is either recycled or unbleached, but not both. Which is better for the environment?

A *Recycling is, ultimately, better for the environment because it involves reusing resources that could become depleted. However, recycling does involve bleaching, and chlorine bleaches release dioxins into rivers, damaging wildlife and the environment. There are, however, recycled toilet papers that do not involve the use of chlorine. If you can't find one, unbleached is best for the environment in terms of pollution, but does create waste problems.*

9 ORGANIC THE WIDER PICTURE

Organic farming has been embraced worldwide by Western countries and by lesser-developed countries that depend heavily on exporting their products to the West. The organic movement is almost entirely consumer-driven and, as demand increases, this has encouraged governments around the world to take note. The international focus on environmental issues has also put organic farming in the spotlight, and an increasing number of countries have now decided that it provides the key to a more certain environmental future. Finally, organic farming has been boosted by the rocketing costs of healthcare, cleaning up pollution, replacing eroded soil and coping with waste and a growing number of superpests that threaten ecosystems on a major scale.

The natural, organic approach offers solutions to a wide variety of problems, including the health of farm workers, environmental pollution, soil erosion, waste build-up and dwindling wildlife. Instead of using chemicals, this pheromone-loaded insect trap attracts male insects that attack cotton plants.

The critics of organic farming are quick to come up with arguments as to why it is not a sustainable alternative to conventional, intensive farming (see pages 124–125), but with increasing demand and the undoubted health and safety aspects coming to the fore, they are being silenced. Almost every country in the Western world is now taking steps to convert at least some of its land to organic farming, and initiatives are in place to standardise the organic guidelines for international and national certification. Most countries aim to improve their organic production, setting targets well into the twenty-first century.

WHY ORGANIC CAN MAKE A DIFFERENCE

All the main benefits that can be obtained from going organic have been discussed in this book, but it is important to summarise here why they will make a real difference on an international level, both

Scandinavian farms are forerunners in the organic stakes, but many other countries around the world are now following suit.

Environmental issues play a major role in the decision by international organisations to embrace the organic philosophy.

for Western countries and for less-developed nations. According to IFOAM (the International Federation of Organic Agricultural Movements, see page 16), organic agriculture:

◆ Includes all the various agricultural systems that promote the environmentally, socially and economically sound production of food and fibres.

◆ Takes local soil fertility as a key to successful production. By respecting the natural capacity of plants, animals and the landscape, these systems aim to optimise quality in all aspects of agriculture and the environment.

◆ Dramatically reduces external input by refraining from the use of chemosynthetic fertilisers, pesticides and pharmaceuticals. Instead it allows the powerful laws of nature to increase both agricultural yields and disease resistance.

◆ Adheres to globally accepted principles, which are implemented within local socio-economic, geo-climatical and cultural settings. As a logical consequence, IFOAM and other organic bodies stress and encourage the development of self-supporting systems at local and regional levels.

A SUSTAINABLE FUTURE

In January 1999 the Food and Agriculture Organisation's Committee on Agriculture (COAG) adopted a report which concluded that many aspects of organic farming were important elements of a system approach to sustainable food production; it also recognised both the environmental and the potential health benefits of organic agriculture, as well as its contribution of innovative production technologies to other agriculture systems and to the overall goals of sustainability.

COAG proposed 'to give the practice associated with organic agriculture a place within sustainable agriculture programmes' and endorsed 'the development of an organisation-wide and cross-sectoral programme in organic agriculture'.

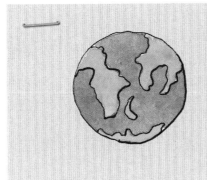

WHAT'S GOING ON IN THE WORLD?

It's official: the organic movement is expanding beyond all predictions, and a huge number of diverse countries are now joining in. Consumer demand is one factor, but the focus on personal responsibility is also playing a part. The following pages show what is going on around the world.

ORGANIC FACTS

🐝 In the US ten million organic consumers will buy $8bn (£5.8bn) of organic food this year. In Europe trends indicate that 30–50 per cent of all farming may be organic by 2010.

🐝 In the UK one of the largest supermarket chains, Tesco, predicts that by 2005 sales of its organic foods will quadruple to £1bn. The Iceland supermarket chain is making a commitment to sell organic produce at the same price as normal and has pledged to help increase organic acreage through a pioneering partnership with the National Trust. At present 70 per cent of organic products sold in the UK are imported.

🐝 Northern-hemisphere developed countries have invested the most money in organic agricultural research. Even so, the contribution is minimal (less than 0.01 per cent of the US Department of Agriculture's research budget is directed towards organic agriculture).

🐝 More than 7 million hectares/18 million acres are now devoted to certified organic agriculture in 130 nations.

WHO IS CONVERTING?

There are currently about 8,000 organic farmers in Germany, and about 7 per cent of its farmland is now organic. The latest figures show that the babyfood market there is almost exclusively certified organic, as is more than 30 per cent of the bread that is sold in and around Munich. Austria has more than 20,000 organic farmers, and organic farming totals 10 per cent of all agricultural land. Sweden and Finland have also experienced rapid growth in this area, while Denmark has set a target of reaching a 20 per cent share of its total food market for organic products in the next couple of years. At present roughly 8 per cent of its agricultural land is farmed organically. But one of the most staggering increases was found in Italy, which went from 18,000 organic farms or conversions in 1996 to 40,000 in 1999.

The acting EU Environment Commissioner Ritt Bjerregaard has proposed that the European Union sets targets for increasing the importance of organic farming in order to reduce the impact of agriculture on the environment. She suggests that the EU triples the area of land that is farmed organically by the year 2005. By the year 2010 the EU will aim for 25 per cent of all its arable land to be organic. In the UK roughly 3 per cent of farmland is now organic, and the Soil Association has set the UK government a challenge of reaching 30 per cent by the year 2010.

In the US the organic food industry has been increasing at a rate of 20 per cent annually over the past decade (rising to around 40 per cent over the past few years). Produce sold by about 12,000 organic farmers in the US will fetch $6bn (£4.1bn). Organic farming became one of the fastest-growing segments of US agriculture during the 1990s. Certified organic cropland more than doubled from 1992 to 1997, and two organic livestock sectors – eggs and dairy – grew even faster. Several states have begun to subsidise conversion to organic farming systems in order to improve the environment. These same initiatives are now taking place in France, Germany and many other EU countries, where organic farmers are being subsidised to reduce pollution.

Less-developed nations are also on course for an organic boom. In Uganda, for instance, 7,000 farmers cultivate organic cotton, and tens of thousands of small farmers in Mexico produce organic coffee and staple goods for local markets. In Egypt organic produce is becoming mainstream. The Egyptian biodynamic SEKEM initiative currently employs about 1,000 staff and delivers its products to 7,000 pharmacies and 2,000 shops. IFOAM also reports rapidly growing consumer demand in Argentina, Japan, Poland and Australia; France, Singapore and Japan are all currently experiencing growth rates at above 20 per cent; and China is experiencing a movement for 'green food' which, according to government grading standards, is produced without certain pesticides and fertilisers and using biological methods. Chinese farmers also produce organic food for export (tea to the Netherlands and the UK, and soya beans to Japan).

Growing interest in organic products in the West has sparked an organic revolution in the Far East, where organic agriculture has grown to meet demand.

115

INTERNATIONAL KITE-MARKS

Although efforts are being made to provide international standards for organic agriculture and production, some countries are way ahead, while others have yet to adopt any organic policies. The IFOAM (see page 16) Accreditation Programme is the only international mechanism currently in existence for conformity assessment of organic certification; its seal (enclosing the world within the letter O) is its mark.

THE EU

Each EU country has its own national organic certification authority, which conforms to EU standards, and within each there are various certification

bodies, which may apply additional specifications. In turn, EU standards are subject to those laid down by IFOAM. The international organic trade fair Biofach (held in Germany each year) has recently produced an EU certification kite-mark, which is available in several languages.

Issues surrounding animal welfare and the problems associated with conventionally farmed meat have created a market for organically reared animals worldwide.

The British Soil Association approves 70 per cent of organic British produce – it is the largest British organic body.

The UK Register of Organic Standards approves and supervises other UK certification bodies. These bodies may also use the UKROFS logo.

IFOAM's main function is to coordinate the network of organic movements around the world.

THE UK

The Soil Association (see pages 15 and 16) is only one of several UK certification boards, but it is the leading authority and governing body. It suggests that you look out for the following:

◆ THE UK REGISTER OF ORGANIC FOOD STANDARDS (UKROFS): largely funded by the Ministry of Agriculture, Fisheries and Food (MAFF), UKROFS is the government authority responsible for the approval and supervision of other certification bodies. Producers registered with the following bodies may also use the UKROFS logo.

◆ SOIL ASSOCIATION CERTIFICATION (SA CERT.): the country's leading certification body certifies approximately 70 per cent of organic food produced in the UK. It operates its own set of standards, which are more specific and generally stricter than UKROFS.

◆ ORGANIC FOOD FEDERATION (OFF): this is a trade federation (see logo on page 16) set up to help its members market organic foods. Its standards conform to UKROFS.

◆ ORGANIC FARMERS AND GROWERS (OF&G): the second-largest organic certification body in the UK (see logo on page 16), its standards also conform to UKROFS.

◆ DEMETER: this is the written symbol used by the Bio-Dynamic Agricultural Association (BDAA, see page 13). Biodynamic agriculture has been described as 'organic plus'.

◆ IRISH ORGANIC FARMERS' AND GROWERS' ASSOCIATION (IOFGA): this association has its own standards, in addition to those laid down by UKROFS.

◆ SCOTTISH ORGANIC PRODUCERS' ASSOCIATION (SOPA): its standards conform to UKROFS.

Although organically farmed land represents only a small percentage of agriculture on a global scale, small farms are already reaping the benefits, and more farmers, faced with serious crises, are showing an interest.

THE US

The Organic Foods Production Act of 1990 (OFPA) authorises the Secretary of Agriculture to approve state organic certification programmes that are consistent with the national organic standards and regulations established under OFPA. However, the new USDA organic bill goes into force in February 2001 and will be fully implemented by August 2002. If a state does not have (or want) a certification programme, then the organic requirements of the USDA's National Organic Program (NOP) will be effective, and will be administered by the NOP office in the USDA.

CANADA

Certification of organic agricultural products in Canada is a voluntary decision. As part of an industry-led initiative proposed in 1996, the certification system under development by the Canadian Organic Advisory Board (COAB) is primarily designed to be consistent with the rapidly evolving requirements of certification bodies for organic

In Canada, although the certification of organic agricultural products, such as cereal crops, is voluntary at present, new trademarks and requirements are being developed.

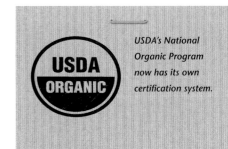

USDA's National Organic Program now has its own certification system.

Demeter is the symbol of the Bio-Dynamic Agricultural Association, 90 per cent of whose produce is organic.

NASAA is Australia's premier organic certifier of organic production and processing.

COAB's Canada Organic Biologique™ mark indicates conformance to the National Standard of Canada for Organic Agriculture.

products entering the international marketplace. The national accreditation body is the Standards Council of Canada, although there are several other bodies. The new Canadian Organic Approved trademark will appear soon.

AUSTRALIA AND NEW ZEALAND

In the late 1980s groups such as the National Association for Sustainable Agriculture Australia (NASAA) were formed by organic growers to certify farms as organic. The government, recognising the export value of organic produce, set up the Organic Produce Advisory Committee (OPAC). This developed a National Standard for Organic and Biodynamic Produce, which must be met by certifying agencies. The Commonwealth Department of Primary Industry (DPI), through its Australian Quarantine Inspection Service (AQIS), has accredited various organic organisations represented on OPAC as capable of carrying out farm certifications. Organic growers' certifying bodies in Australia currently include: the Organic Vignerons' Association of Australia Inc.; Demeter (BDAA); Bio-Dynamic Farming & Gardening Association; Biological Farmers of Australia; National Association for Sustainable Agriculture; Organic Food; Bio-Dynamic Research Institute.

One of the recent changes to the management of the National Standard was the closing down of OPAC in early 1999. In its place is the Organic Produce Export Committee (OPEC). This is chaired by AQIS and has a change to its terms of reference, as its name implies. OPEC will focus on export issues such as market access, rather than the detail of standard development.

There are no national standards in New Zealand, although they will eventually agree standards with Australia. They use the Bio-Gro and Demeter labels for organic certification.

In Australia various different organisations exist to make consumers aware of the benefits of chemical-free food and to encourage the adoption of organic farming systems.

ORGANIC
THE WIDER
PICTURE

QUESTIONS
& ANSWERS

Q Organic gardening seems to be rather backward in an age of growing technology. Isn't there any other solution?

A *Don't be fooled. Organic organisations incorporate the best of cutting-edge technology in their assessments of appropriate techniques, and these are amended as more viable solutions arise. Going back to nature may seem idealistic, but studies show that it does provide what world agriculture really needs: sustainable farming, producing safe food, using methods that enhance the natural environment.*

Q Will the cost of organic goods come down as demand increases?

A *According to the laws of supply and demand, the costs will certainly come down. However, organic farming will always be more expensive (see page 124) because of the costs involved in producing high-quality goods. And there is another issue that needs to be considered here: cheap food tends to cause us to undervalue its importance. Good-quality food is an essential part of life, and paying a little more for something so significant may cause us to take our diets and our consumption a little more seriously.*

Q Are governments taking organic farming and production seriously?

A *Governments around the world have set targets and national organic standards. In the UK, a bill was put forward in 1999 which aims to ensure that, by January 2010, no less than 30 per cent of agricultural land in England and Wales is certified as organic or is in the process of being converted to that status, and not less than 20 per cent by volume of food consumed is certified as organic. Denmark has set a target of becoming 20 per cent organic over the next few years, and Japan is establishing its first national organic standards.*

Q Will the organic import/export market increase with production?

A *Undoubtedly, and although this has environmental implications (see page 122), it does encourage the use of sustainable organic farming methods in less developed countries, which may not otherwise have considered them. With more money being poured into organic agriculture at national levels, however, there will be an increase in the varieties produced within home markets. Big business demands trade between other countries, and even something as idealistic as the organic movement cannot hope to seriously dent that.*

Q What is the most important reason to choose organic?

A *Health is probably the number-one reason, and this extends from people through wildlife to the environment – and everything within it. There are other important issues, such as feeding the world and protecting rural communities, but better health is the main reason why consumers are going organic, and they are right to do so. The past decade has highlighted major problems with conventional farming methods, including pesticides, BSE, BST, hormones and food poisoning. Organic is the solution to these problems.*

Q How can we help to encourage the organic movement?

A *Buy organic, grow organic in your garden, join an organic association in your local area or country, support local growing schemes, farmers' markets, delivery services and farms, and express your commitment to the cause by spreading the news. You don't have to be boring to educate your friends, family and colleagues about the benefits of the organic movement, and the more people we get on board, the better it is for everyone.*

Q Why haven't more people chosen to go organic?

A *Although the industry is growing, and consumer education is increasing, there are still many people who are unaware of the real costs of conventional farming and production, including those that affect health and the environment. In fact, the majority of people who do choose organic are unaware of issues such as sustainable farming, biodiversity and soil erosion. However, as more and more people are converted, the good news will spread and consumption will continue to increase.*

Q Why haven't more farmers decided to go organic?

A *There are cost implications: typically farmers experience some loss in yields after converting to organic production, and it may take years to restore the ecosystem. There is also a two- or three-year period in which farmers are in 'no man's land', before certification. And most studies have found that organic agriculture requires greater labour input than conventional farming. But the greatest problem seems to be lack of information and support in the farming industry. This should change as more funding becomes available for education and research.*

Q If an organic product isn't certified, does that mean it isn't really organic?

A *The likelihood is that it isn't. Farmers who use organic methods have an incentive to get their products certified, as such goods are considered superior by the consumer. Furthermore, most farmers take great pride in the fact that they have used organic methods and are pleased to advertise the fact. However, certification is voluntary, and some producers simply do not bother. If a producer has a good track record and can prove their organic approach, you may decide to choose uncertified products.*

Q Why do some certified organic companies produce goods that are not certified organic?

A *Organic guidelines cover not only ingredients, but many other criteria, such as processing and production methods and transport. It may be that one product in a range fails to meet one of these criteria. Be aware that manufactured products often contain certified ingredients, but the processing itself may not be certified.*

10 NOBODY'S PERFECT

Anyone who chooses to live organically will face inevitable criticism and conjecture about the organic movement. But remember this: although organic farming and production are still in their infancy, forming at present only a very small percentage of agricultural land around the world, they do pose a real threat to conventional methods. Why? Because the organic movement has sprung directly from the demands of consumers themselves, who have become literally sick of the problems that are associated with food, chemicals and environmental threats.

When a small number of what most people considered to be 'cranks' can change the way we feel about food, farming and processing practices, there is nothing short of a revolution afoot. Big business stands to lose a lot of money as the organic movement grows, and you can be certain that opposition will spring up from all quarters.

THE DOWNSIDE

It is, however, important to remember that the organic solution is not perfect. It undoubtedly has disadvantages, the greatest of which is cost – that is, cost to the consumer, and cost to the farmer, who faces lower yields, much more expensive and time-consuming manual labour and at least a two-year period before they can be certified. There are also problems associated with importing, although this is essential in some cases, if consumer demand is to be met. First, it threatens the organic ethic by making it more difficult to regulate, by creating pollution and by making things harder for local farmers. Second, importing organic foods creates fundamental problems, because the preservatives and other chemicals and techniques used in the conventional farming industry to prevent rotting cannot be applied to organic products. It is obvious that you cannot expect to deliver fresh organic produce halfway around the world without some compromises being made. One of these is the use of ethylene on bananas.

This chapter looks at some of the drawbacks of the organic movement and presents the views of both the critics and the lobbyists. But problems can always be overcome, and the organic movement is embracing the positive benefits of technology and science. The undoubtedly worthy aims of organic farming, production and living may not be the solution to world hunger now, for example, but they may be in the future. What is important is that organic living engenders a positive spirit for change that will benefit the planet and everything within it.

Even the most idealistic
consumer would find it
difficult to sustain a
wholly organic lifestyle.
But remember:
everything you do
helps the cause.

THE MIDDLE WAY

In the end, every consumer has a choice. But with the best intentions in the world, it may be impossible to go completely organic (see pages 124–125). It is great to be idealistic and to plan to devote time and energy to living organically, but sometimes this just is not possible. There is nothing worse than turning your garden over to organic production, only to find it ridden with pests and full of inedible produce. We are used to quick-fix solutions, and it may take time and lots of patience to embrace methods of growing, producing and living that do not satisfy our demands immediately.

It might be difficult for a busy mother, for example, to choose and cook her own organic babyfoods, while also breastfeeding her child, serving nutritious organic meals to her family, keeping her garden free of pests naturally, washing the organic cotton nappies, recycling products and making her own shampoos. Something has to give along the way, and opting out may be an easy choice. But remember that everyone has the responsibility to make an effort to preserve the environment and their health. If you are only able to do that in small ways, you will still be making a significant difference, and if everybody thought along the same lines, then that difference would be enormous.

Finding a middle road is the way forward for most people. Remember that every step along that road helps the environment, prevents the inhumane treatment of animals, enhances biodiversity, helps to protect the health of wildlife and humans alike, encourages a sustainable way of life and helps to guarantee our children a healthy future in an untainted world.

Supporting organic agricultural methods can help to protect the safety of farmers in developing countries.

There are solutions for consumers (see page 128), but it is worth considering in greater detail the issues of cost. There is mounting evidence that if all the indirect costs of conventional food production (the clean-up of polluted water, replacement of eroded soils, cost of healthcare for farmers and their workers, plus consumers) were factored into the price of food, then organic foods would actually cost the same, or even be cheaper. For example, the price of meat would double or triple if the full ecological costs – including fossil-fuel use, ground-water depletion and agricultural-chemical pollution – were factored in.

THE DRAWBACKS OF GOING ORGANIC

There are undoubtedly some drawbacks to going organic, on both a personal and a global level, and organic organisations will be the first to admit that things have not reached the stage where they are perfect yet. Here are the main issues, with an idea of how things might change in the future.

COST

Organic food is certainly more expensive and the average consumer may have difficulty meeting this. But costs are coming down, although organic food is always likely to cost more than conventional food. There are many reasons for this, but the most salient ones are the fact that more labour is required, less food is produced per hectare/acre and stringent controls mean that corners simply cannot be cut – anywhere.

INCONVENIENCE

This may be a temporary problem, but many consumers find it difficult to locate organic products. Organic living also involves a great deal of label-reading (although it does not take long for a well-practised eye to locate a kite-mark on packaging), plus shopping at different venues and organisations.

Foods go off more quickly (see page 45) without conventional preservatives, and for a busy household this can be frustrating, expensive and, yet again, time-consuming. Ideally organic produce should be purchased several times a week to guarantee peak freshness and nutritional value. That is not always an option for some consumers. However, the industry is booming, and even fairly remote communities now have access to box schemes, mail-order deliveries and the Internet. Consumer demand will increase that access even further in the future.

POOR SELECTION

Unless you are prepared to cough up money for imported organics, you have to rely on what might be a fairly limited local market. Not everyone is naturally adventurous, and the prospect of choosing and using unfamiliar products may be daunting to some consumers. However, farmers are beginning to experiment with organic imported seed to produce non-native varieties locally. Furthermore, you can expect to see variety grow in other products as the market expands.

CONSUMER WARINESS

Most consumers are wary of trends, largely because manufacturers are so keen to cash in on them. If organic becomes big business, then there is the potential for the high ideals to be diluted when money becomes a factor. At the present time there is no risk of this, and international agencies have been set up to protect the values of the industry. But already canny manufacturers are cashing in on the organic name (see page 62), which can make things confusing and misleading for consumers.

Not surprisingly, many people would rather risk the conventional 'devil they know' than be duped into paying up to twice the price for something that isn't what it says it is. And because 'organic' has become synonymous with health, consumers are obviously confused when they find organic cigarettes, colas and sweets lining supermarket shelves (see pages 126–127). These contradictions tend to undermine the industry, making consumers wary. But remember some of the issues: the average child receives four times more exposure than an adult to at least eight widely used cancer-causing pesticides in food. The majority of farmers in the Western world are facing an unprecedented crisis. Organic farming could be one of the few sustainable ways to ensure that small farms can survive.

Cost is an obvious drawback to eating organic, particularly for families on tight budgets. However, the savings made on cleaning up pollution and treating health problems will eventually bring down the price.

125

An organic cigarette? It's certainly lower in chemicals that can be detrimental to health, and some people believe that it is a viable alternative. However, smoking is known to cause lung cancer and a variety of other health conditions, whether you smoke organic or not.

Choosing organic 'treats' means that you are getting fewer of the chemical ingredients known to cause health problems. However, they should never take the place of good, fresh and healthy organic food.

THE BIG CONTRADICTIONS: ARE WE BEING CONNED BY THE TERM 'ORGANIC'?

The birth of the 'unhealthy' organic product movement is a cause for concern. It is easy to see where the problem lies. For example, if your diet is based on refined products (white bread, biscuits and cakes), tinned foods, red meat, sweets, crisps, soft drinks and chocolate, you will not be getting the nutrients you need for health and well being. As all of these products are now available organically, it is perfectly possible to have an unhealthy organic diet.

The basis of health is the same, whether you choose organic products or not. You need to aim for good-quality complex carbohydrates in the form of wholegrains, unrefined cereals and rice. Fruit, vegetables, lean meat, pulses and other vegetable proteins, a little dairy produce and plenty of fresh water complete the picture. Alcohol needs to be kept to a minimum, and smoking is known to cause lung cancer and a host of other diseases, whether or not you choose organic cigarettes.

SOME OF THE ANOMALIES

ORGANIC CHOCOLATE: chocolate is not as bad for you as you might think. It is high in sugar, caffeine and saturated fats, but it does contain iron and other minerals, plus theobromine, which triggers the release of natural 'feel-good' chemicals in the brain. Conventional chocolate is made from heavily sprayed cocoa beans, and the use of pesticides and other chemicals is poorly regulated. Good-quality organic chocolate contains 60–70 per cent cocoa solids (about 20 per cent in milk chocolate), less sugar, no hydrogenated fats and none of the extra chemicals.

ORGANIC WINE (see page 47): non-organic vines are chemically fertilised and sprayed against oidium, mildew and the cochilis moth. In the Mediterranean region herbicides are sprayed on them to eliminate grass and weeds, which absorb vital moisture. Organic wine, beer, cider, ale and spirits are produced without chemical fertilisers, nitrates, organophosphates, herbicides, artificial colourings, fungicides and GMOs. They are a better bet, but only within reason!

ORGANIC CRISPS AND OTHER SNACKS: the junk-food market has been overwhelmed by genetically modified organisms in recent years, and this is one very good reason to choose organic (see pages 30–31). Flavoured conventional brands contain a horrifying number of artificial ingredients. While organic brands could never be considered 'nutritious', they are a viable alternative.

ORGANIC CIGARETTES: organic tobacco-growers must conform to the same strict guidelines as any other organic farmer, which means that the use of agrochemicals is out of the question. Given that conventional tobacco plants are heavily sprayed, you will be cutting down on a wide variety of noxious chemicals by smoking organic. Some 600 additives can legally be added to tobacco products, but this number is substantially reduced in organic brands.

SOFT DRINKS: (see pages 46–47).

DO POOR ORGANIC PRODUCTS HAVE ANY BENEFITS?

Organic products are always a better choice, because they do not contain the toxic chemicals and other constituents associated with conventional farming methods and because of the environmental implications, which cannot be overlooked. So if biscuits form a staple part of your diet, then it is best to choose organic. Smoking cannot be condoned in any book that focuses on health, but if you do smoke, then organic cigarettes are free of many of the toxic chemicals associated with most ordinary brands. So even a poor organic diet can reduce the number of toxic chemicals in your body, which may affect your health.

But these products do not in themselves encourage health, or do anything to ensure that your body systems are working at an optimum level. They are not nutritious, and they may take the place of key nutrients in your diet, which might be disastrous in the long term. An organic diet is only 'healthy' if it contains all the elements of a healthy diet. Biscuits and other treats are acceptable if they form only a small proportion and do not replace essential nutritious foods.

127

FINDING A MIDDLE ROAD

Some consumers find the prospect of going completely organic daunting and cost-prohibitive. But remember, it's not an 'all or nothing' movement. Anything organic that you add to your diet, any organic methods that you use in your garden, any organic product that you choose over a conventional alternative will make a positive contribution to the industry. It will help to encourage the demand for products that consider the welfare of people, plantlife, wildlife and the planet itself.

One of the key principles is the concept of balance – ensuring that the natural balance is maintained to encourage the health of everything within nature. This concept can be applied to your own life, too. If you cannot afford to eat all-organic food, for example, you can make a big difference to your health by balancing the bad with the good, the unhealthy with the healthy. Broadly speaking, if 80 per cent of your diet is healthy and largely organic, you can get away with a bit more in the other 20 per cent.

GRADUAL CHANGE

Take things slowly, introducing organic products to your diet one at a time. For instance, choose a time to clear out your snack cupboard, then replace the products one by one with healthier organic alternatives. Work out what you can afford, based on the foods you eat most frequently and the danger foods (see box). Experiment with different purchasing methods: you may find that a box scheme of fruit and vegetables delivered every week cuts down substantially on your supermarket requirements. By choosing vegetable protein in place of meat, you might make your budget work. Give yourself a target to change different parts of your diet: one week meat, the next tinned goods, and so on. You will gradually learn how and where to get the most affordable, healthy organic options.

If you are having a baby or you have small children, you may already have begun the transition to healthier organic eating, and now is a good time to try some organic solutions around the house. Once again, take it slowly. Replace your dishwasher detergent with an organic brand. Simply purchase organic or good-quality green and environmentally friendly brands as you need them. Then take a look at personal hygiene. A small bottle of organic essential oil, such as lavender, can be used in the bath, as an insecticide, an air freshener, an antibacterial cleaner and a natural aid to relaxation. Look at the options before you purchase the products you have always used and which you buy as a matter of course.

Indulge yourself in organic alternatives to conventional beauty products. It's easy to implement a few changes that will make a big difference to your overall health.

IF YOU HAVE TO CHOOSE ...

BABYFOOD: the Washington-based Environmental Working Group (EWG) commissioned laboratory tests of eight baby foods made by industry leaders. Some 16 different pesticides were found, including three carcinogens (cancer-causing agents), five possible carcinogens, eight neurotoxins, five endocrine disrupters (which can mimic or interfere with hormones) and five very dangerous 'toxicity one' chemicals. More than half of the samples – 53 per cent – had detectable pesticide levels.

STRAWBERRIES: according to a 1993 study, strawberries are the single most heavily contaminated fruit or vegetable in the US. The picture is no different in other countries.

RICE: an incredible 70–80 per cent of the world's calories come from rice. Because rice allergies are practically non-existent, rice is a primary ingredient in baby cereals and snacks. Both water-soluble herbicides and insecticides are used on rice, which affects not only consumer health, but also our ground-water.

OATS AND OTHER GRAINS: oats are a fundamental grain in crop rotation, and they are used by farmers to maintain soil health and to break pest cycles. However, studies have now found that illegal chemical residues are present in many oat products. All cereals have small grains, which means that they absorb more agrochemicals per weight.

MILK: BST, antibiotics, growth hormones, GMOs in dairy feed (see pages 30–31, 42 and 50–51) . . . Always choose organic.

CORN: about 50 per cent of all pesticides, by weight, are applied to corn in the US. While corn has only 5 per cent of the pesticide contamination of strawberries (see left), it is found in a huge variety of different products and is a dietary staple in the West and in many poor areas of the world.

BANANAS: toxic pesticides used during banana production include benomyl (which has been linked to birth defects) and chlorpyrifos (a neurotoxin). In Costa Rica, a major banana exporter, only 5 per cent of cultivated land is taken up with bananas, but they actually account for 35 per cent of the country's total pesticide imports.

GREEN BEANS: the US Environmental Protection Agency has registered more than 60 pesticides for use on green beans, including neurotoxins and endocrine (hormone) disrupters.

PEACHES: a recent Food and Drug Administration study in the US cited peaches for above-average rates of illegal pesticide violations (5 per cent of the crop was contaminated). Peaches are heavily sprayed with the dangerous pesticide pronamide.

APPLES: domestic US apples have more than 65 per cent as much pesticide contamination as strawberries, and that is after the heavily publicised 1980s' US battle that banned use of the carcinogenic growth regulator Alar. Some 48 pesticides are commonly used on apples.

LAUNDRY DETERGENTS: most of these are an ecological nightmare, containing phosphates that encourage the growth of algae, which is choking our waterways and killing local plant, marine and animal life. Shop for detergents containing sodium carbonate or sodium citrate instead.

GROWING ORGANIC

Almost anyone can have fun with organic gardening, whether your garden is a single window box or your home backs onto a meadow. Start by choosing organic seed and by using natural pest protection, such as soft-soap sprays and slug traps. Give up buying anything that does not have 'certified organic' stamped on it. You will soon find alternative methods, and the process can be enjoyable. You will learn to understand the ecosystem within your garden, and will feel safer allowing your children to play in a space untainted by chemicals. And every family with a reasonable plot should have a compost heap.

Every element of the natural world, including plants, animals, insects and soil, works together to create a harmonious cycle in the garden, upon which each organism grows and then thrives. Even the most seasoned gardener cannot fail to be intrigued by the diversity of an organic garden.

TOP TEN TIPS FOR ORGANIC LIVING

Having studied all the issues in connection with organic production, and having looked at everything from organic food and gardening methods to personal-hygiene and household products, we can now establish the top ten tips for organic living – wherever you are, and however large or small your budget.

1 Choose as much organic food as you can find and afford. If you have to choose, make fruit and vegetables, milk, grains and meat your first priority.

2 Invest in or create a compost heap. It offers a great way to reduce and recycle waste, and a natural means of fertilising your garden.

3 Consider the cleaning products in your store cupboard and decide what you really need. Only replace the essentials, and use natural organic alternatives for the remainder (see pages 104–105). Do the same with your body-care products, cosmetics and toiletries. Choose those without chemical ingredients, and read the labels carefully.

4 Investigate the organic possibilities in your area, searching out local farmers, co-operatives, box schemes and mail-order delivery services.

5 Stop using chemicals in your home and garden wherever possible. Choose organic, environmentally friendly and certified 'green' products, or experiment with the natural alternatives that have been suggested throughout this book.

6 Educate yourself, your family and your friends about the positive benefits of going organic. Everyone who takes part increases the demand, brings down the cost and encourages a healthier way of living.

7 Replace fabrics with organic cotton or hemp in your home as they come up for renewal. Organic clothing, bedding, towels and many other products are now available and not prohibitively expensive.

8 Overhaul your diet, cutting out chemicals, refined and junk foods wherever possible. You will look and feel better, and the cost of your weekly shopping will reduce substantially. Incorporate organic foods for enhanced health benefits. Above all, make sure you use cooking methods that preserve the nutrition and quality of your food.

9 Seek out organic restaurants, B&Bs, farms and events for the whole family. Create a well-rounded, healthy lifestyle for yourself and your children.

10 Have fun and further the cause! Support the anti-GM lobby, read up on the subject, join organisations that promote organic living.

FURTHER READING

BOOKS AVAILABLE IN THE UK

LUKE ANDERSON, *Genetic Engineering, Food and Our Environment*, Green Books, 1999

FRANCES BISSELL, *The Organic Meat Cookbook*, Ebury Press, 1999

JOANNA BLYTHMAN, *The Food Our Children Eat*, Fourth Estate, 2000

LYNDA BROWN, *The (New) Shopper's Guide to Organic Food*, Fourth Estate, 1998, 2000

SUE DIBB AND DR TIM LOBSTEIN, *GM Free: A Shopper's Guide to Genetically Modified Food*, Virgin Books, 1999

JOHN ELKINGTON AND JULIA HAILES, *The Green Consumer Guide*, Gollancz, 1987

JOHN ELKINGTON AND JULIA HAILES, *The New Foods Guide*, Gollancz, 1999

BOB FLOWERDEW, *Bob Flowerdew's Complete Book of Companion Gardening*, Kyle Cathie, 2000

BOB FLOWERDEW, *Bob Flowerdew's Organic Bible: Successful Gardening the Natural Way*, Kyle Cathie, 1998

BOB FLOWERDEW, *The Organic Gardener*, Kyle Cathie, 1994 (paperback edition 1998)

DR MARILYN GLENVILLE, *Natural Health Solutions for Women*, Piatkus Books, 2001

PIPPA GREENWOOD, *Pippa's Organic Kitchen Garden*, Dorling Kindersley, 1999

GEOFF HAMILTON, *DK Pocket Encyclopaedia of Organic Gardening*, Dorling Kindersley, 1991

COLIN HINES, *Localization – A Global Manifesto*, Earthscan, 2000

PATRICK HOLFORD, *Optimum Nutrition Bible*, Piatkus Books, 1998

CLIVE LITCHFIELD, *The Organic Directory 2000/2001* (UK), Green Books, 2000

TERRY MARSHALL, *Organic Tomatoes – The Inside Story*, Harris Associates, 1999

DEBORAH L. MARTIN (ed.), *The Rodale Book of Composting: Easy Methods for Every Gardener*, Rodale Press, 1992

TANYIA MAXTED-FROST, *The Organic Baby Book*, Green Books, 1999

PAULINE PEARS, *All About Compost: Recycling Household and Garden Waste*, HDRA/Search Press, 1999

JO READMAN, *Soil Care and Management*, Soil Association, 1991

ANNA ROSS, *Green Cuisine: The Organic Vegetable Cookbook*, Green Peppercorn, 1999

JOHN RULAC, *Backyard Composting*, Green Books, 1998

ROGER SCRUTON, *Animal Rights and Wrongs*, Metro Books, 2000

GORDON STRONG (ed.), *A Gardener's Guide to Organic Gardening*, Merehurst, 2000

KAREN SULLIVAN, *Natural Healthcare for Children*, Piatkus Books, 2000

MARIA THUN, *Gardening for Life: the Biodynamic Way*, Hawthorn Press, 1999

MICHAEL VAN STRATEN, *Organic Super Foods*, Mitchell Beazley, 1999

MONTY WALDIN, *Friends of the Earth Organic Wine Guide*, Thorsons, 1999

HILARY WRIGHT, *The Great Organic Wine Guide*, Piatkus Books, 2000

BOOKS AVAILABLE IN THE US

C. COLSTON BURRELL, *A Gardener's Encyclopedia of Wildflowers: An Organic Guide to Choosing and Growing over 150 Beautiful Wildflowers*, Rodale Press, 1997

KARAN DAVIS CUTLER et al., *Burpee: The Complete Vegetable & Herb Gardener: A Guide to Growing Your Garden Organically*, DG Books, 1997

TANYA DENCHLA, *The Organic Gardener's Home Reference: A Plant-By-Plant Guide to Growing Fresh, Healthy Food*, Storey Books, 1994

STUART FRANKLIN et al., *Building a Healthy Lawn: A Safe and Natural Approach*, Storey Books, 1988

JAMES BERNARD FROST, *The Artichoke Trail: A Guide to Vegetarian Restaurants, Organic Food Stores & Farmers' Markets in the US*, Hunter, 2000

JOHN B. HARRIS, *Growing Food Organically*, Waterwheel Press, 1993

MIKE MCGRATH (ed.), *The Best of Organic Gardening: Over 50 Years of Organic Advice and Reader-Proven Techniques from America's Best-Loved Gardening Magazine*, Rodale Press, 1996

DEBORAH L. MARTIN AND SALLY JEAN CUNNINGHAM (eds), *1001 Ingenious Gardening Ideas: New, Fun, and Fabulous Tips That Will Change the Way You Garden – Forever!*, Rodale Press, 1999

RHONDA MASSINGHAM HART, *Bugs, Slugs & Other Thugs: Controlling Garden Pests Organically*, Storey Books, 1991

CATHERINE PALADINO, *One Good Apple: Growing Our Food for the Sake of the Earth*, Houghton Mifflin, 1999

MICHAEL PHILLIPS, *The Apple Grower: A Guide for the Organic Orchardist*, Chelsea Green Publishing, 1998

ROB PROCTOR, *Annuals and Bulbs (Rodale's Successful Organic Gardening)*, St Martin's Press, 1995

LOUISE SECRETS, *Carrots Love Tomatoes: Secrets of Companion Planting for Successful Gardening*, Storey Books, 1998

ROGER YEPSEN (ed.), *1001 Old-Time Garden Tips: Timeless Bits of Wisdom on How to Grow Everything Organically, from the Good Old Days When Everyone Did*, Rodale Press, 1998

MAGAZINES AND PERIODICALS

02 Zone (UK)

100% Health (UK)

Ethical Consumer Magazine (UK)

The Food Magazine (published by the Food Commission, UK)

GM Free (UK)

Growing Organically (the HDRA magazine; UK)

Here's Health (UK)

The Inside Story (UK)

Natural Product News (UK)

Optimum Nutrition (journal of the Institute of Optimum Nutrition, UK)

Organic Gardening (UK)

Organic Gardening (US)

Organic Living (UK)

Organic Living (US)

Permaculture Magazine (UK)

Pesticides News (UK)

Positive News (UK)

What Your Doctor Doesn't Tell You (US & UK)

PUBLICATIONS AVAILABLE FROM THE ORGANIC TRADE ASSOCIATION, US (SEE PAGE 136)

IFOAM Directory: Organic Agriculture Worldwide 1998/9

Organic Fibre Directory: more than 200 listings of growers, mills, designers, retailers, and so on, plus hard-to-find market information

The Organic Pages: 1999 North American Resource Directory: listings for every sector of the organic industry, including farmers, certification agencies, manufacturers, distributors, brokers, importers, exporters, fibre products, and so on

Taste Life! The Organic Choice: features 20 essays about organic agriculture from contributors such as Robert Rodale, Frank Ford, Walt Whitman, Wendy Gordon and Grace Grershuny

PUBLICATIONS AVAILABLE FROM CANADIAN ORGANIC GROWERS (SEE PAGE 134)

Organic Field Crop Handbook

Organic Livestock Handbook

USEFUL ADDRESSES

USEFUL INTERNATIONAL WEBSITES

ALTERNATIVE FARMING SYSTEMS INFORMATION CENTER (AFSIC)

http://www.nal.usda.gov/afsic/afslinks.htm

AFSIC is one of several US topic-oriented information centres at the National Agricultural Library (Maryland), supported, in part, by the USDA's Sustainable Agriculture Research and Education (SARE) programme. AFSIC specialises in locating and accessing information related to alternative cropping systems, including sustainable, organic, low-input, biodynamic and regenerative agriculture.

AUSTRALIA NATIONAL STANDARDS

http://www.bfa.com.au/frames/national.htm

Australian national standards for organic and biodynamic produce.

BIODYNAMIC FARMING AND GARDENING ASSOCIATION (BDA)

http://www.biodynamics.com/

Provides information on biodynamic farming, related education (training, apprenticeship opportunities, calendars), food (links to Demeter-certified products list and biodynamic food mail-order service), discussion forum, conferences, literature and advice.

CANADIAN ORGANIC GROWERS (COG)

http://www.gks.com/cog/

COG is the national information network for organic gardeners, farmers and consumers in Canada. The site provides information on its organisation and membership, events, publications and news, an online resource library, a message board (for discussions), an eco-market database of growers, products and services, job and apprenticeship opportunities.

CANBERRA ORGANIC GROWERS' SOCIETY (COGS)

http://www.netspeed.com.au/cogs/cogsabt.htm

The aim of this Australian non-profit-making organisation is to provide 'a forum for organic growers to exchange information, and encourage the general public to adopt organic growing methods'. The page offers a wide range of general information on organic farming, selected articles, web-links (Australia, USA and others), etc.

CODEX ALIMENTARIUS COMMISSION

http://www.fao.org/WAICENT/FAOINFO/ECONOMIC/ESN/codex/STANDARD/standard.htmFAO/WHO

Guidelines on the production, processing, labelling and marketing of organically produced foods.

DANISH INSTITUTE OF AGRICULTURAL SCIENCES

http://www.sp.dk/~jph/Areas/Organic_Farming/organic_farming.html

DANISH ORGANIC

http://www.ecoweb.dk/english/

Provides information on Danish institutions and organisations; facts on organic farming in Denmark.

DOCUMENTATION OF ECOLOGICAL AGRICULTURE (DOCEA)

http://www.bib.wau.nl/docea/

DOCEA is an initiative of the European Network for Scientific Research Coordination in Organic Farming (ENOF), which aims at concerted action through various documentation centres and user-representatives, for a better availability of literature relevant to ecological agriculture.

ECOLOGICAL AGRICULTURE PROJECTS (EAP)

http://eap.mcgill.ca/general/home_frames.htm

Canada's leading resource centre for sustainable agriculture.

EU ORGANIC REGULATION

http://europa.eu.int/comm/sg/consolid/en/391r2092/artm.htm

Council regulation

EUROPEAN INITIATIVE FOR AGRICULTURAL RESEARCH FOR DEVELOPMENT (EIARD)

http://www.eiard.org

An information and communication system whose objective is to moderate hot topics in agricultural research for development.

EUROPEAN INITIATIVE FOR AGRICULTURAL RESEARCH FOR DEVELOPMENT INFOSYS

http://www.dainet.de/eiard/infosys/europa/frameset_hot_topics.htm

EUROPEAN NETWORK FOR SCIENTIFIC RESEARCH COORDINATION IN ORGANIC FARMING (ENOF)

http://www.cid.csic.es/enof/

The objective of ENOF, funded by the Commission of the European Communities and managed by the Direction General of Agriculture (DG VI), is to put in contact and establish collaborations in the field of education, research, experimentation, demonstration and diffusion of organic farming techniques within Europe.

HENRY A. WALLACE INSTITUTE FOR ALTERNATIVE AGRICULTURE

http://www.hawiaa.org

The Institute aims to 'encourage and facilitate the adoption of low-cost, resource-conserving and environmentally sound farming systems' by providing 'the leadership and policy research and analysis necessary to influence national agricultural policy'. The site contains an overview of programmes, projects and publications on sustainable agriculture, including organic agriculture documents and an analysis of the US National Organic Program proposed rule.

INSTITUTE OF ORGANIC AGRICULTURE

(University of Bonn, Germany)

http://www.uni-bonn.de/iol/english.htm

LAND, LIVESTOCK AND ENVIRONMENT

http://www.geocities.com/RainForest/Canopy/3770/aslam.htm

Provides an electronic journal (with several organic agriculture features) and links to diverse aspects of land utilisation, including organic farming, EU-organic, organic Net and organic herbs.

ORGANIC CONSUMERS' ASSOCIATION (OCA)

http://www.organicconsumers.org/

OCA is a US consumer advocacy organisation promoting organic food and fibre production and affiliated with the Campaign for Food Safety. The page provides book reviews (mainly on food safety), lists of US and Canadian food co-operatives and community-supported agriculture farms (by state), green pages, an eco-directory and sources of organic fertilisers, list of events, links and facts about organic agriculture, food safety and organic standards, OCA projects and other information.

ORGANIC COTTON

http://www.sustainablecotton.org/

The site includes an exhibit featuring cotton-industry history, information on farming organic cotton, related production and processing procedures, directories, as well as description of a sustainable cotton project and organic cotton farm tours.

ORGANIC FARMERS' MARKETING ASSOCIATION (OFMA)

http://web.iquest.net/ofma/

The US OFMA 'assists organic farmers in marketing, communication and public advocacy. In the spirit of such co-operation, this website has been created to bring together organic farmers, consumers and supporters of organic agriculture from all over the world.'

ORGANIC FARMING RESEARCH FOUNDATION (OFRF)

http://www.ofrf.org

US site with information about organic agriculture, special events, procedures for grant application, OFRF-funded research, policy programme, results, an information bulletin, farming conference calendar, financial support, web links (rich list of sites related to research and education, policy and government, organisations, farming in general, marketing information, soil, water, pesticides and web surfing).

ORGANIC GRAPES INTO WINE ALLIANCE (OGWA)

http://www.isgnet.com/ogwa

Includes standards for wines produced from organic grapes and certified growers in the US.

ORGANIC TRADE ASSOCIATION (OTA)

http://www.ota.com

OTA represents the organic industry in Canada and the United States. Members include growers, shippers, processors, certifiers, farmer associations, brokers, consultants, distributors and retailers. Established in 1985 as the Organic Foods Production Association of North America, OTA now works to promote organic products in the marketplace and to protect the integrity of organic standards. The web page presents information about the organisation and organic subjects; a publications list with an order form; news and trends; links; events and opportunities; a list of suppliers; and a directory for organic needs.

ORGANIC TRADING AND INFORMATION CENTRE

http://www.organicfood.com/

An international site for consumers and producers of organic foods and natural products. The site contains information on organic markets, operating companies and organisations, an information library, buy/sell offers of products; and free listing possibilities.

RESEARCH INSTITUTE OF ORGANIC AGRICULTURE (FIBL)

http://www.fibl.ch/

Swiss research institution involved in research projects on soils, plants, livestock, landscape and biodiversity, economics and standards.

SCOTTISH AGRICULTURAL COLLEGE (SAC)

http://sac004.ed.sac.ac.uk/cropsci/external/ORGANIC/default.htm

Contains information on the SAC Organic Farming Centre and Farms, and its research projects.

SOIL ASSOCIATION

http://www.soilassociation.org

The Soil Association is the UK's leading campaigning and certification body for organic food and farming. The site contains information on activities and campaigns, publications, organic food and international forestry certification.

WELSH INSTITUTE OF RURAL STUDIES

http://www.wirs.aber.ac.uk/research/organic.shtml

The Welsh Institute is at the University of Wales, Aberystwyth. It offers Organic Farming and Agro-ecology pages, including graphs detailing the number of farms, land area and proportion of the agricultural sector in different European countries since 1985.

US NATIONAL ORGANIC PROGRAM

http://www.ams.usda.gov/nop/index.htm

The Agricultural Marketing Service (AMS) of the United States Department of Agriculture (USDA) informs about the National Organic Program and comments on issues.

INTERNATIONAL ORGANIC GARDENING AND FARMING ASSOCIATIONS

AGROECOLOGY PROGRAM

Steve Gliessman, University of California, Santa Cruz, CA 95064, USA
fax: (408) 2867/2799

HENRY DOUBLEDAY RESEARCH ASSOCIATION OF AUSTRALIA (HDRA)

R.B. McNeill, 816 Comleroy Road, AUS-Kurrajong, NSW 2758, Australia
tel: (45) 761220
http://www.hdra.asn.au/

ILEIA/ETC – FOUNDATION

Win Hiemstra, Kastanjelaan 5, PO Box 64, NL-3830 AB Leusden, The Netherlands
tel: (33) 4943086
fax: (33) 4940791

IRISH ORGANIC FARMERS' AND GROWERS' ASSOCIATION (IOFGA)

56 Blessington Street, Dublin 7, Irish Republic
tel: (018) 307996
fax: (018) 300925

LOUIS BOLK INSTITUTE

I. Te Velde, Hoofdstaat 24, NL-3972 LA Driebergen, The Netherlands
tel: (3438) 17814
fax: (3438) 15611

NATURE ET PROGRÈS
Patrick Barré, 3 Place Pasteur, F-840000
Avignon, France
tel: (4) 90 827846
fax: (4) 90 829728

**ORGANIC GROWERS' ASSOCIATION OF NEW
SOUTH WALES (OGA-NSW)**
Cecil Bodnar, 49 South Liverpool Road,
AUS-Heckenberg, NSW 2168, Australia
tel: (2) 8250078

ORGANIC TRUST LIMITED
Offer a professional, user-friendly inspection and
certification service for organic food products
in Ireland.
Vernon House, 2 Vernon Avenue, Clontarf,
Dublin 3, Irish Republic
tel/fax: (1) 853 0271
e-mail: organic@iol.ie
http://www.iol.ie/~organic/trust.html

RODALE INSTITUTE
Anthony Rodale, 222 Main Street, Emmaus,
PA 18049, USA
tel: (610) 6831400
fax: (610) 6838548

TERRE VIVANTE
Karin Mundit, Dom de Raud, BP 20,
F-38711 Mens Cedex, France
tel: (4) 76 348080
fax: (4) 76 348080

**VERBAND FÜR ORGANISCH-BIOLOGISCHEN
LANDBAU (BIOLAND)**
Hans-Jörg Däuwel, Postfach 208, D-73002
Göppingen, Germany
tel: (7161) 910120
fax: (7161) 910127

BRITISH AND EUROPEAN ASSOCIATIONS

APPLIED RURAL ALTERNATIVES
10 Highfield Close, Wokingham,
Berks RG40 1DG, UK

BIO-DYNAMIC AGRICULTURAL ASSOCIATION
Painswick Inn Project, Gloucester Street, Stroud,
Gloucester GL5 1QG, UK
tel/fax: (01453) 759501

COMMUNITY COMPOSTING NETWORK
67 Alexandra Road, Sheffield S2 3EE, UK
tel/fax: (0114) 258 0483
e-mail: ccn@gn.apc.org
http://www.chiron-s.demon.co.uk/ccn

COMPASSION IN WORLD FARMING
Charles House, 5A Charles Street, Petersfield,
Hants GU32 3EH, UK
tel: (01730) 264208
fax: (01730) 260791
e-mail: compassion@ciwf.co.uk
http://www.ciwf.co.uk

**DEMETER STANDARDS COMMITTEE OF THE
BIO-DYNAMIC AGRICULTURAL ASSOCIATION**
17 Inverleith Place, Edinburgh EH3 5QE, UK
tel: (0131) 624 3921

FOOD COMMISSION
94 White Lion Street, London N1 9PF, UK
tel: (020) 7837 2250
fax: (020) 7837 1141
e-mail: foodcomm@compuserve.com
http://www.foodcom.org.uk

FRIENDS OF THE EARTH
26–28 Underwood Street, London N1 7JQ, UK
tel: (020) 7490 1555
fax: (020) 7490 0881
e-mail: info@foe.co.uk
http://www.foe.co.uk

GENETICS FORUM
94 White Lion Street, London N1 9PF, UK
tel: (020) 7837 9229
fax: (020) 7837 1141
e-mail: geneticsforum@gn.apc.org
http://www.geneticsforum.org.uk

GREENPEACE UK
Canonbury Villas, London N1 2PN, UK
tel: (020) 7865 8100
fax: (020) 7865 8200
e-mail: gp-info@uk.greenpeace.org
http://www.greenpeace.org.uk

**HENRY DOUBLEDAY RESEARCH
ASSOCIATION (HDRA)**
Ryton Organic Gardens, Ryton on Dunsmore,
Coventry CV8 3LG, UK
tel: (02476) 303517
fax: (02476) 639229
e-mail: rog@hdra.org.uk
http://www.hdra.org.uk

**INTERNATIONAL FEDERATION OF ORGANIC
AGRICULTURE MOVEMENTS (IFOAM)**
c/o Ökozentrum Imsbach, D-66636 Tholey-
Theley, Germany
tel: (6853) 919890
fax: (6853) 919899
e-mail: HeadOffice@ifoam.org
http://www.ifoam.org

**NATIONAL ASSOCIATION
OF FARMERS' MARKETS**
South Vaults, Green Park Station, Green Park
Road, Bath BA1 1JB, UK
tel: (01225) 787914
fax: (01225) 460840

NORFOLK ORGANIC GARDENERS
6 Old Grove Court, Norwich NR3 3NL, UK
tel: (01603) 403415
e-mail: norfolkorganic@cwcom.net
http://www.norfolkorganic.mcmail.com

ORGANIC FARM CENTRE,
Harbour Road, Kilbeggan, County West Meath,
Irish Republic
tel: 0506 32563
fax: 0506 32063
e-mail: iofga@tinet.ie
http://www.irishorganic.ie

ORGANIC FARMERS AND GROWERS LTD
The Elin Centre, Lancaster Road,
Shrewsbury SY1 3LE, UK
tel: (01743) 440512
fax: (01743) 461481

ORGANIC FARMERS SCOTLAND
Block 2, Unit 4, Bandeath Industrial Estate,
Throsk, Stirling FK7 7XY, UK
tel: (02786) 817581
fax: (01786) 816100
e-mail: enquiries@organicfrmssco.demon.co.uk

ORGANIC FOOD FEDERATION
Unit 1, Manor Enterprise Centre, Mowles Manor,
Etling Green, Dereham NR20 3EZ, UK
tel: (01362) 637314
fax: (01362) 637980

**SCOTTISH ORGANIC PRODUCERS'
ASSOCIATION (SOPA)**
Milton of Cambus, Doune, Perthshire
FK16 6HG, UK
tel/fax: (01786) 841657
e-mail: contact@sopa.demon.co.uk

SOIL ASSOCIATION
Bristol House, 40–56 Victoria Street,
Bristol BS1 6BY, UK
tel: (0117) 929 0661
fax: (0117) 925 2504
e-mail: info@soilassociation.org
http://www.soilassociation.org

**UNITED KINGDOM REGISTER OF ORGANIC
FOOD STANDARDS (UKROFS)**
Nobel House, 17 Smith Square, London
SW1P 3JR, UK
tel: (020) 7238 5915

**WILLING WORKERS ON ORGANIC FARMS
(WWOOF)**
PO Box 2675, Lewes, East Sussex BN7 1RB, UK
tel/fax: (01273) 476286
e-mail: fran@wwoof-k.freeserve.co.uk
http://www.phdc.com/wwoof

AUSTRALIAN ASSOCIATIONS
**ORGANIC RETAILERS' & GROWERS' ASSOCIATION
OF AUSTRALIA (ORGAA)**
PO Box 12852, A'Beckett Street, Post Office,
Melbourne, VIC 3000
hotline: 1800 356 299
ORGAA is a unique nationwide organisation with
a membership consisting of growers, retailers and
environmentally aware consumers. It was formed
in 1986 in response to a growing concern
regarding our food-production systems.

AUSTRALIAN CERTIFYING BODIES

BIO-DYNAMIC FARMING & GARDENING ASSOCIATION

PO Box 54, Bellingham, NSW 2454

tel/fax: (02) 6655 8551

e-mail: poss@midcoast.com.au

BIO-DYNAMIC RESEARCH INSTITUTE

Main Road, Powelltown, VIC 3797

tel: (03) 5966 7333

fax: (03) 5966 7433

BIOLOGICAL FARMERS OF AUSTRALIA (BFA)

PO Box 3404, Toowoomba Village Fair,

Toowoomba, QLD 4350

tel: (07) 4639 3299

fax: (07) 4639 3755

DEMETER (BIO-DYNAMIC AGRICULTURE ASSOCIATION (BDAA)

Main Road, Powelltown, VIC

tel: (03) 5966 7370 / fax: (03) 5966 7339

NATIONAL ASSOCIATION FOR SUSTAINABLE AGRICULTURE AUSTRALIA (NASAA)

PO Box 768, Stirling, SA 5152

tel: (08) 8370 8455 / mobile: 019 692 217

fax: (08) 8370 8381

e-mail nasaa@dove.mtx.net.au

http://www.nasaa.com.au

ORGANIC HERB GROWERS OF AUSTRALIA INC.

PO Box 6171, South Lismore, NSW 2480

tel: (02) 6622 0100

e-mail: admin@organicherbs.org

ORGANIC FOOD CHAIN

PO Box 2390, Toowoomba, QLD 4350

tel: (07) 4637 2600

fax: (07) 4696 7689

e-mail: organicfoodchain@hotmail.com

ORGANIC VIGNERONS' ASSOCIATION OF AUSTRALIA INC.

PO Box 503, Nuriootpa, SA 5355

tel: (08) 8562 2122

fax: (08) 8562 3034

e-mail boss@dove.net.au

NEW ZEALAND ASSOCIATIONS

AGRIQUALITY NEW ZEALAND LTD

Sandra Walker, PO Box 82, Wanganui

tel: (6) 348-5870 / mobile: 025 518 247

e-mail: WalkerS@agriquality.co.nz

http://www.agriquality.co.nz

AgriQuality New Zealand provides an organic certification service to organic producers and processors. AgriQuality has 58 offices throughout New Zealand providing national coverage with a professional, efficient and competitive service. It also provides advice to those wishing to 'go organic'.

THE BIO-DYNAMIC FARMING AND GARDENING ASSOCIATION (DEMETER)

David Wright, PO Box 390 45,

Wellington Mail Centre, Wellington

tel: (+64) (4) 589 5366

fax: (+64) (4) 589 5365

e-mail: d.wright@clear.net.nz

BIO-GRO NEW ZEALAND

PO Box 9693, Marion Square, Wellington

tel: (4) 801-9741

fax: (4) 801-9742

e-mail: info@bio-gro.co.nz

http://www.bio-gro.co.nz

BIO-GRO New Zealand is the trading name of the NZ Biological Producers' & Consumers' Council Inc., an organisation formed in 1983 as a non-profit-making Incorporated Society. It is the registered owner of the BIO-GRO trademark and has developed a set of production standards for organic agriculture, which are internationally recognised and respected. BIO-GRO New Zealand is the leading organic certification agency in New Zealand and an accredited member of the International Federation of Organic Agriculture Movements (IFOAM), based in Germany.

SOUTH AFRICAN ASSOCIATIONS

ZA-BIO-DYNAMIC AGRICULTURAL ASSOCIATION SOUTHERN AFRICA (DEMETER)

PO Box 115, ZA-2056, Paulshof

tel/fax: (11) 803 7191

INDEX

ACKNOWLEDGEMENTS

The publishers would like to thank the following for the use of pictures. Every effort has been made to trace copyright holders and obtain permission. The publishers apologise for any omissions and would be pleased to make any necessary changes at subsequent printings.

CORBIS: 119, 124, /Adrian Arbib 31, /Michael Boys 71, /Lowell George 30, /Richard Hamilton Smith 7, /Robert Holmes 59, /Hulton Deutsch 15, /Jacqui Hurst 60, /Kevin King: Ecoscene 32, /Michael Lewis 44, /Dennis Marsico 113, /Kevin R.Morris 123, /Richard T. Nowitz 48, 58, 112, /Roger Ressmeyer 49, /Joel W. Rogers 84, /Martin Rogers 56, /John Wilkinson: Ecoscene 50.

LIZ EDDISON: 72, 76, 77, 79, 117, 130.

HULTON GETTY: 12, 14.

STOCKMARKET: 18, 19, 25, 34, 92, 95, 96, 106, 126.

TONY STONE: 27, 40, /Lori Adamski Peek 24, 99, /Chris Baker 36T /Roy Botterell 9, /Dugald Bremner 68, /Christopher Burki 73, /Laurie Campbell 103, /Stewart Cohen 8, /Thomas Del Brase 2, 54, /Mark Douet 86, /Fisher: Thatcher 108, /Paul Greliunas 115, /Pat Hermansen 6, /Gary Holscher 46, /G. Brad Lewis 66, /Mark Lewis 10, /Liz McCaulay 62, /Laurence Monneret 104, /Kevin Morris 118, /Graeme Norways 43,

/Ian O'Leary 88, /PBJ Pictures 125, /Andre Perlstein 26T, /Andy Sacks 21, 116, /Ken Scott 128, /Bob Thomas 97, /John Turner 82.

A huge number of organizations supplied invaluable information for this book. The author would like to acknowledge the assistance of the following: Friends of the Earth, The Soil Association, Henry Doubleday Research Association, Organic Consumers Association, US Department of Agriculture, UK Ecolabelling Board, National Association for Sustainable Agriculture Australia (NASAA), DEMETER (Bio-Dynamic Agriculture Association (BDAA), Organic Retailers & Growers Association of Australia, Organic Trust Limited, Irish Organic Farmers and Growers Association. (IOFGA), The Canadian Organic Advisory Board (COAB), Simply Food, Canadian Organic Growers, Henry A. Wallace Institute for Alternative Agriculture, Canberra Organic Growers Society (COGS), Organic Cotton, Organic Grapes into Wine Alliance (OGWA), Organic Trade Association (OTA), Organic Farmers Marketing Association (OFMA), Research Institute of Organic Agriculture (FiBL), European Network for Scientific Research Coordination in Organic Farming (ENOF), Willing Workers on Organic Farms (WWOOF), United Kingdom Register of Organic Food Standards (UKROFS), Organic Food Federation, Greenpeace UK, Community Composting Network, and International Federation of Organic Agriculture Movements (IFOAM).

Thanks also to Caroline Earle for help and support throughout the project, and to Gill Bailey, who saw the potential for the book.